the hummingbird bakery

HOME SWEET HOME

Tarek Malouf
and The Hummingbird Bakers

Collins

CONTENTS

INTRODUCTION

Ever since the first Hummingbird Bakery opened in Notting Hill, west London, in 2004 it has been amazing to see how many people have enjoyed our cakes and treats. That they have also been inspired to bake at home, however, is something that we never expected. The popularity of home baking has grown so much since our ovens were first turned on, which is something that makes us extremely happy. So for *Home Sweet Home*, our third cookbook, we decided to celebrate classic home baking with best-loved flavours and nostalgic recipes – all of which come with our distinctive American-inspired Hummingbird Bakery twist, of course!

America has a rich heritage of home baking, handed down from generation to generation, never ashamed of being sweet, indulgent or brash. But there's also a down-to-earth quality about American baking, never needing to be overly fussy or putting style before flavour.

We've gone a step further in *Home Sweet Home*, bringing you a whole range of delicious goodies, including creative cupcakes like the tangy Key Lime or quirky Doughnut; simple cookies, such as the melt-in-the-mouth Chocolate Truffle; impressive but easy-to-make desserts, including the eye-catching Red Velvet Roulade and divine Peanut Butter Cheesecake; classic fruit cobblers and some of the most indulgent pies you'll ever come across – the Candy Bar is our absolute favourite! Some cupcakes from our daily specials make an appearance too, such as Rhubarb & Custard and Popcorn from our old-fashioned sweets and carnival ranges.

Most people know us for our sweet things, but sometimes a savoury bake is called for when cooking at home. So we've provided some easy savoury recipes that make ideal snacks or party nibbles. From weekend comfort home baking and biscuit tin treats to impressive special occasion cakes, *Home Sweet Home* includes a wonderful variety of recipes.

We do hope you enjoy our latest offering and that it gives you the perfect excuse to dust off the weighing scales, fire up your oven and get that mixer buzzing!

Tarek

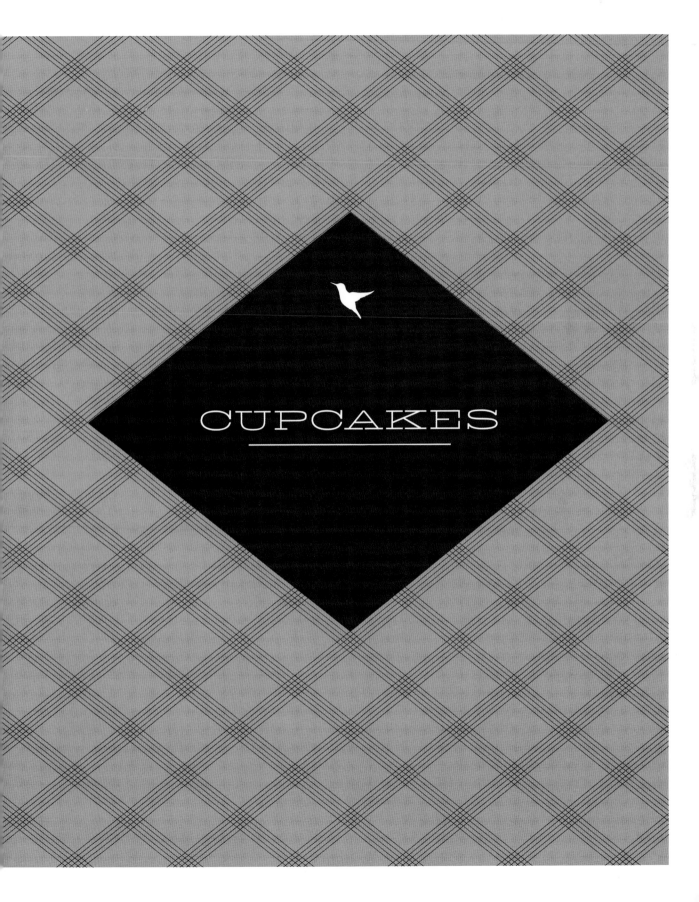

CUPCAKES

This is one of the most popular flavours from our biscuit tin range. The tangy orange marmalade goes so well with the sponge and chocolate frosting. You can decorate the top with mini Jaffa Cakes or cut up normal-sized ones if you prefer.

Jaffa Cake Cupcakes

MAKES 12–16 CUPCAKES

FOR THE SPONGE

70g (2½ oz) UNSALTED BUTTER, SOFTENED

210g (7½ oz) PLAIN FLOUR

250g (9oz) CASTER SUGAR

1 tbsp BAKING POWDER

½ tsp SALT

210ml (7½ fl oz) WHOLE MILK

2 LARGE EGGS

1 tsp VANILLA EXTRACT

100g (3½ oz) SMOOTH ORANGE MARMALADE

FOR THE FROSTING

450g (1lb) ICING SUGAR, SIFTED

60g (2oz) COCOA POWDER, SIFTED

150g (5½ oz) UNSALTED BUTTER, SOFTENED

60ml (2fl oz) WHOLE MILK

MINI JAFFA CAKES, TO DECORATE

EQUIPMENT

ONE OR TWO 12-HOLE DEEP MUFFIN TINS

1. Preheat the oven to 170°C (325°F), Gas mark 3, and line the muffin tins with paper muffin cases to make the number you require.

2. First make the sponge. In a freestanding electric mixer with the paddle attachment or using a hand-held electric whisk, mix the butter, flour, sugar, baking powder and salt together until they form a crumb-like consistency.

3. In a jug, mix together the milk, eggs and vanilla extract by hand.

4. With the mixer or whisk on a slow speed, gradually pour half the liquid into the flour and butter and mix thoroughly until combined. Turn up the speed and beat until the batter is smooth and thick with no lumps. Scrape down the sides of the bowl as you go along. Once any lumps are gone, turn the speed back down and gradually pour in the rest of the liquid, continuing to mix until smooth and combined.

5. Spoon the batter into the prepared paper cases, filling them two-thirds full. Using a 50ml (1¾ fl oz) ice-cream scoop can make this process easier and will result in even cupcakes.

6. Bake for 20–25 minutes or until the cupcakes are golden brown and the sponge bounces back when lightly touched. Leave to cool slightly before removing from the tins and placing on a wire rack to cool completely before frosting.

7. Using a freestanding electric mixer with the paddle attachment or a hand-held electric whisk, gradually mix the icing sugar, cocoa powder and butter together on a low speed until combined and there are no large lumps of butter. Gradually add the milk while mixing on a slow speed. Once incorporated, increase the speed and beat until light and fluffy.

8. Once the cupcakes are cool, use a sharp knife to make a hollow in the centre of each cupcake, approximately 2cm (¾in) in diameter and about 3cm (1¼in) deep. Retain the cut-out piece of sponge. Spoon about 1–2 teaspoons of orange marmalade into the hollow. Replace the cut-out piece of sponge, trimming to fit and pressing down gently to ensure that the top is level with the rest of the cake.

9. Spoon a generous amount of the frosting onto each cupcake, then gently smooth over with a palette knife, making a swirl at the top if you wish. Top each cupcake with a mini Jaffa Cake.

Mint and caramel combine beautifully together to recreate this old-fashioned boiled sweet in cupcake form. They can also be dusted with mint-flavoured fudge if you can't find real mint humbugs.

Mint Humbug Cupcakes

MAKES 12–16 CUPCAKES

FOR THE SPONGE

70g (2½oz) UNSALTED BUTTER, SOFTENED

210g (7½oz) PLAIN FLOUR

250g (9oz) CASTER SUGAR

1 tbsp BAKING POWDER

½ tsp SALT

210ml (7½fl oz) WHOLE MILK

½ tsp PEPPERMINT ESSENCE

2 LARGE EGGS

50g (1¾oz) TINNED CARAMEL OR *DULCE DE LECHE*

FOR THE FROSTING

500g (1lb 2oz) ICING SUGAR, SIFTED

160g (5½oz) UNSALTED BUTTER, SOFTENED

50ml (1¾fl oz) WHOLE MILK

¼ tsp PEPPERMINT ESSENCE

20g (¾oz) TINNED CARAMEL OR *DULCE DE LECHE*

6 MINT HUMBUG SWEETS, ROUGHLY CHOPPED INTO BITS, TO DECORATE

EQUIPMENT

ONE OR TWO 12-HOLE DEEP MUFFIN TINS

1. Preheat the oven to 170°C (325°F), Gas mark 3, and line the muffin tins with paper muffin cases to make the number you require.

2. First make the sponge. In a freestanding electric mixer with the paddle attachment or using a hand-held electric whisk, mix the butter, flour, sugar, baking powder and salt together until they form a crumb-like consistency.

3. In a jug, mix together the milk, peppermint essence and eggs by hand.

4. With the mixer or whisk on a slow speed, gradually pour in half of the liquid and mix thoroughly until combined. Raise the speed to medium and beat until the batter is smooth and thick, with no lumps. Scrape down the sides of the bowl from time to time. Once all lumps are gone, turn the speed back down and gradually pour in the remaining liquid, continuing to mix until the batter is smooth and combined.

5. Add the *dulce de leche* and mix, making sure it is evenly incorporated into the batter.

6. Spoon the batter into the prepared paper cases, filling them two-thirds full. Using a 50ml (1¾fl oz) ice-cream scoop can make this process easier and will result in even cupcakes. Bake for 20–25 minutes or until the sponge bounces back when lightly touched. Leave to cool slightly before removing from the tin and placing on a wire rack to cool completely before frosting.

7. Using a freestanding electric mixer with the paddle attachment or a hand-held electric whisk, gradually mix the icing sugar and butter together on a low speed until combined and there are no large lumps of butter. In a jug, mix the milk and peppermint essence together. Gradually pour the milk into the butter and icing sugar, while mixing on a slow speed. When all the liquid is incorporated, turn the mixer up to a high speed and beat the frosting until light and fluffy.

8. Add the *dulce de leche* and mix through the frosting until even and smooth.

9. Spoon generous amounts of the frosting onto each cupcake, then gently smooth over with a palette knife, making a swirl at the top if you wish. Top each cupcake with a sprinkling of the chopped mint humbug sweets.

Part of our carnival range, this indulgent cupcake takes you straight to the fairground. It's very tempting to eat the warm mini doughnuts as they come out of the pan … or just make some extra ones for baker's perks!

Doughnut Cupcakes

MAKES 12–16 CUPCAKES

FOR THE SPONGE

70g (2½oz) UNSALTED BUTTER, SOFTENED

210g (7½oz) PLAIN FLOUR

250g (9oz) CASTER SUGAR

1 tbsp BAKING POWDER

½ tsp SALT

210ml (7½fl oz) WHOLE MILK

2 LARGE EGGS

100g (3½oz) STRAWBERRY JAM

FOR THE CINNAMON SUGAR

1 tsp GROUND CINNAMON

100g (3½oz) CASTER SUGAR

FOR THE DOUGHNUTS

250g (9oz) PLAIN FLOUR, PLUS EXTRA FOR DUSTING

¼ tsp SALT

½ tsp BAKING POWDER

35g (1¼oz) COLD UNSALTED BUTTER, CUBED

35g (1¼oz) CASTER SUGAR

1 LARGE EGG

125ml (4½fl oz) WHOLE MILK

1 LITRE (1¾ pints) SUNFLOWER OIL

Ingredients continue …

1. Preheat the oven to 170°C (325°F), Gas mark 3, and line muffin tins with paper muffin cases to make the number you require.

2. First make the sponge. In a freestanding electric mixer with the paddle attachment or using a hand-held electric whisk, mix the butter, flour, sugar, baking powder and salt together until they form a crumb-like consistency.

3. In a jug, mix together the milk and eggs by hand.

4. With the mixer or whisk on a slow speed, gradually pour in half of the liquid and mix thoroughly until combined. Raise the speed to medium and mix until the batter is smooth and thick, with no lumps. Scrape down the sides of the bowl occasionally. Once all lumps are gone, turn the speed back down and gradually pour in the remaining liquid, continuing to mix until the batter is smooth and combined.

5. Spoon the batter into the prepared paper cases, filling them two-thirds full. Using a 50ml (1¾fl oz) ice-cream scoop can make this process easier and will result in even cupcakes.

6. Bake for approximately 20–25 minutes or until golden brown and the sponge bounces back when lightly touched. Leave to cool slightly before removing from the tin and placing on a wire rack to cool completely before frosting.

7. While the cakes are baking, make the cinnamon sugar and doughnuts. In a small bowl, mix the cinnamon and caster sugar together and set aside. Sift the flour, salt and baking powder together in a medium bowl. Using your fingertips, rub in the butter until the mixture forms rough crumbs. Add the sugar and mix through.

8. In a separate jug, mix the egg and milk together by hand. Make a well in the middle of the crumb mixture. Pour the liquid into the well and mix all the ingredients together to form a dough.

Recipe continues …

FOR THE FROSTING

660g (1lb 7oz) ICING SUGAR, SIFTED

1 tsp GROUND CINNAMON

210g (7½oz) UNSALTED BUTTER, SOFTENED

60ml (2fl oz) WHOLE MILK

EQUIPMENT

ONE OR TWO 12-HOLE DEEP MUFFIN TINS

1–2cm (½–¾in) ROUND COOKIE CUTTER

SUGAR THERMOMETER

9. Line a baking tray with baking parchment. On a lightly floured surface, roll out the dough to about 1cm (½in) thick. Using the cutter, cut out small round doughnuts. Place the doughnut balls onto the prepared tray.

10. Line another baking tray or large plate with kitchen paper. In a large pan, heat up the oil to 140–160°C (275–320°F).

11. Using a slotted spoon carefully place the doughnut balls into the oil, one at a time. Don't put more than 10 doughnuts in at a time. Fry the doughnuts until they are an even golden brown. When the doughnuts are done, carefully take them out of the oil using a slotted spoon and place them on the prepared kitchen paper to cool slightly. Once cooled, roll the doughnuts in the cinnamon sugar, making sure they are completely coated.

12. Using the freestanding electric mixer with the paddle attachment or the hand-held electric whisk, make the frosting by gradually mixing the icing sugar, ground cinnamon and butter together on a low speed until combined and there are no large lumps of butter. Gradually pour the milk into the butter and icing sugar while mixing on a slow speed. When all the liquid is incorporated, turn the mixer up to a high speed and beat the frosting until light and fluffy.

13. Once the cupcakes are cool, use a sharp knife to make a hollow in the centre of each cupcake, approximately 2cm (¾in) in diameter and about 3cm (1¼in) deep. Retain the cut-out piece of sponge. Spoon about 1 teaspoon of the jam into the hollow. Replace the cut-out piece of sponge, trimming to fit and pressing down gently to ensure that the top is level with the rest of the cake.

14. Spoon generous amounts of the frosting onto each cupcake, then gently smooth over with a palette knife, making a swirl at the top if you wish. Top each cupcake with a small doughnut ball.

* If you don't have a thermometer to check the oil in the pan is hot enough, drop a croûton-sized piece of white bread into the oil and it should go golden brown within 10 seconds. If it goes brown too early, reduce the heat and drop in another piece of bread. If it takes too long to turn brown then let the oil heat up a little more.

One Christmas we decided to mix things up and created this Italian biscuit-inspired recipe as an alternative to our Raspberry Trifle Cupcakes. You can put a tiny dash of amaretto liqueur onto the crushed biscuits if you want something boozier, but be careful not to get them too soggy.

Blueberry & Amaretti Trifle Cupcakes

MAKES 12–16 CUPCAKES

FOR THE SPONGE

70g (2½oz) UNSALTED BUTTER, SOFTENED

210g (7½oz) PLAIN FLOUR

1 tbsp BAKING POWDER

½ tsp SALT

250g (9oz) CASTER SUGAR

210ml (7½fl oz) WHOLE MILK

2 LARGE EGGS

1 tsp VANILLA EXTRACT

150g (5½oz) BLUEBERRIES

FOR THE CUSTARD

330ml (11½fl oz) WHOLE MILK

3 LARGE EGG YOLKS

60g (2oz) CASTER SUGAR

20g (¾oz) PLAIN FLOUR

20g (¾oz) CORNFLOUR

150ml (5½fl oz) DOUBLE CREAM

FOR THE DECORATION

75g (2½oz) BLUEBERRIES

50g (1¾oz) AMARETTI BISCUITS, CRUSHED INTO CRUMBS

EQUIPMENT

ONE OR TWO 12-HOLE DEEP MUFFIN TINS

1. Preheat the oven to 170°C (325°F), Gas mark 3, and line the muffin tins with paper muffin cases to make the number you require.

2. First make the sponge. In a freestanding electric mixer with the paddle attachment or using a hand-held electric whisk, mix the butter, flour, baking powder, salt and sugar together until they form a crumb-like consistency.

3. In a jug, mix together the milk, eggs and vanilla extract by hand.

4. With the mixer or whisk on a slow speed, gradually pour half of the liquid into the crumb mixture and mix thoroughly until combined. Turn up the speed to medium and beat until the batter is smooth and thick, with no lumps. Scrape down the sides of the bowl occasionally. Once all the lumps have been beaten out, turn the speed back down and gradually pour in the remaining liquid from the jug, continuing to mix until the batter is smooth and completely combined. Stir the blueberries into the cake batter by hand.

5. Spoon the batter into the prepared paper cases, filling them two-thirds full. Using a 50ml (1¾fl oz) ice-cream scoop can make this process easier and will result in even cupcakes.

6. Bake for approximately 20–25 minutes or until golden brown and the sponge bounces back when lightly touched. The blueberries will sink into the sponge — this is normal. Leave to cool slightly before removing from the tin and placing on a wire rack to cool completely before frosting.

7. While the cakes are in the oven, make the custard. Place the milk in a saucepan and bring to the boil. In a bowl, mix together the egg yolks, sugar, flour and cornflour to make a paste, adding 1 tablespoon of the hot milk to thin if necessary.

Recipe continues ...

8. When the milk has boiled, remove the pan from the heat and mix 4–5 tablespoons with the egg and flour paste, then pour this back into the pan with the remaining hot milk and return to the heat.

9. Bring back up to the boil, whisking constantly, and continue to boil for a further 3–4 minutes to ensure the flour and cornflour are fully cooked. However, be careful not to overcook or the eggs may begin to scramble. Remove from the heat and immediately pour the custard into a baking tray. Cover straight away with cling film and set aside to cool completely.

10. To finish the custard, pour the double cream into a medium bowl. Using a freestanding electric mixer with the whisk attachment or a hand-held electric whisk, beat the cream until it forms soft peaks. Place the cooled custard into a medium bowl. Using the mixer or whisk, on a slow speed mix the custard until it is smooth. Using a spatula, gradually fold the whipped cream into the custard.

11. Spoon generous amounts of the custard onto each cupcake, then gently smooth over with a palette knife, making a swirl at the top if you wish. Top each cupcake with 3–4 blueberries and a sprinkling of amaretti biscuit crumbs.

This recipe is fantastic for those with a little more time to spare.
We like to make the little biscuit decorations for the top, but you can use shop-bought mini Jammie Dodgers or other jam-filled shortbread biscuits.

Jolly Jammer Cupcakes

MAKES 12–16 CUPCAKES

FOR THE COOKIES

100g (3½oz) UNSALTED BUTTER, SOFTENED

140g (5oz) CASTER SUGAR

1 EGG

200g (7oz) PLAIN FLOUR, PLUS EXTRA FOR DUSTING

¼ tsp CREAM OF TARTAR

FOR THE SPONGE

70g (2½oz) UNSALTED BUTTER, SOFTENED

210g (7½oz) PLAIN FLOUR

250g (9oz) CASTER SUGAR

1 tbsp BAKING POWDER

½ tsp SALT

210ml (7½fl oz) WHOLE MILK

2 LARGE EGGS

1 tsp VANILLA EXTRACT

FOR THE FROSTING

660g (1lb 7oz) ICING SUGAR, SIFTED

210g (7½oz) UNSALTED BUTTER, SOFTENED

60ml (2fl oz) WHOLE MILK

½ tsp VANILLA EXTRACT

Ingredients continue ...

1. Preheat the oven to 170°C (325°F), Gas mark 3, and line a baking tray with baking parchment.

2. To make the cookies, put the butter and sugar in a freestanding electric mixer with the paddle attachment or use a hand-held electric whisk and cream until light and fluffy. Add the egg and mix until fully incorporated.

3. In a small bowl, sift the flour and cream of tartar together. Add the dry ingredients to the butter and egg mixture. Mix on a slow speed until a dough forms. Don't overmix.

4. Roll the dough out on a lightly floured surface to about 3–4mm (⅛in) thick. Using the cookie cutter, cut out 32 (or more) cookies. Then use the piping nozzle or a small sharp knife to make smaller holes in the centres of half the cookies (these will be the cookie tops). Carefully place them all on the prepared baking tray. Any excess dough can be made into more cookies or frozen and used again at a later stage.

5. Bake the cookies for approximately 10–13 minutes or until they start to go a golden brown around the edges. Set aside to cool completely for later use. Leave the oven turned to 170°C (325°F), Gas mark 3.

6. Meanwhile make the sponge. Line the muffin tins with paper muffin cases to make the number you require. In a freestanding electric mixer with the paddle attachment or using a hand-held electric whisk, mix the butter, flour, sugar, baking powder and salt together until they form a crumb-like consistency.

7. In a jug, mix together the milk, eggs and vanilla extract by hand.

8. With the mixer or whisk on a slow speed, gradually pour in half of the liquid and mix thoroughly until combined. Raise the speed to medium and mix until the batter is smooth and thick, with no lumps. Scrape down the sides of the bowl occasionally. Once any lumps are gone, turn the speed back down and gradually pour in the remaining liquid, continuing to mix until the batter is smooth and combined.

Recipe continues ...

FOR THE DECORATION

100g (3½oz) SMOOTH STRAWBERRY JAM

EQUIPMENT

3½cm (1½in) ROUND, FLUTED COOKIE CUTTER

1cm (½in) PIPING NOZZLE

2 PIPING BAGS

ONE OR TWO 12-HOLE DEEP MUFFIN TINS

9. Spoon the batter into the prepared paper cases, filling them two-thirds full. Using a 50ml (1¾fl oz) ice-cream scoop can make this process easier and will result in even cupcakes.

10. Bake for approximately 20–25 minutes or until the cupcakes are golden brown and the sponge bounces back when lightly touched. Leave to cool slightly before removing from the tin and placing on a wire rack to cool completely before frosting.

11. Using the freestanding electric mixer with the paddle attachment or the hand-held electric whisk, gradually mix the icing sugar and butter together on a low speed until combined and there are no large lumps of butter. Gradually pour in the milk and vanilla extract while mixing on a slow speed. When all the liquid is incorporated, turn the mixer up to a high speed and beat the frosting until light and fluffy.

12. To assemble the mini cookies for decoration, place a small amount of the prepared frosting into a piping bag. Gently heat the strawberry jam in a pan over a low heat until it is smooth and slightly melted. Put a small amount of the strawberry jam in a second piping bag.

13. On a tray, lay out the cookies without the holes in the centres. Pipe a small amount of frosting onto each cookie, and a small amount of strawberry jam into the centre. Top each one with a cookie top with a hole in its centre to create a mini 'jolly jammer' sandwich cookie.

14. Once the cupcakes are cool, use a sharp knife to make a hollow in the centre of each cupcake, approximately 2cm (¾in) in diameter and about 3cm (1¼in) deep. Retain the cut-out piece of sponge. Spoon about 1 teaspoon of the frosting into the hollow. Then top with 1 teaspoon of strawberry jam, reheated if necessary to make it smooth and spoonable. Replace the cut-out piece of sponge, trimming to fit and pressing down gently to ensure that the top is level with the rest of the cake.

15. Spoon a generous amount of the frosting onto each cupcake, then gently smooth over with a palette knife, making a swirl at the top if you wish. Top each cupcake with a mini jolly jammer sandwich cookie.

Chocolate and coconut are a perfect flavour combination. Decorate these cupcakes with pieces of coconut chocolate bars or mini versions if you have them to hand.

Chocolate & Coconut Cupcakes

MAKES 12–16 CUPCAKES

FOR THE SPONGE

70g (2½oz) UNSALTED BUTTER, SOFTENED

170g (6oz) PLAIN FLOUR

250g (9oz) CASTER SUGAR

50g (1¾oz) COCOA POWDER, SIFTED

1 tbsp BAKING POWDER

½ tsp SALT

210ml (7½fl oz) WHOLE MILK

2 LARGE EGGS

2–3 COCONUT CHOCOLATE BARS (SUCH AS BOUNTY)

FOR THE FROSTING

500g (1lb 2oz) ICING SUGAR, SIFTED

160g (5½oz) UNSALTED BUTTER, SOFTENED

60ml (2fl oz) COCONUT MILK

FOR THE DECORATION

1–2 COCONUT CHOCOLATE BARS (SUCH AS BOUNTY)

60g (2oz) DESICCATED COCONUT

EQUIPMENT

ONE OR TWO 12-HOLE DEEP MUFFIN TINS

1. Preheat the oven to 170°C (325°F), Gas mark 3, and line the muffin tins with paper muffin cases to make the number you require.

2. First make the sponge. In a freestanding electric mixer with the paddle attachment or using a hand-held electric whisk, mix the butter, flour, sugar, cocoa powder, baking powder and salt together until they form a crumb-like consistency.

3. In a jug, mix together the milk and eggs by hand.

4. With the mixer or whisk on a slow speed, gradually pour in half of the liquid and mix thoroughly until combined. Raise the speed to medium and beat until the batter is smooth and thick, with no lumps. Scrape down the sides of the bowl now and then. Once all lumps are gone, turn the speed back down and gradually pour in the remaining liquid, continuing to mix until the batter is smooth and combined.

5. Spoon the batter into the prepared paper cases, filling them two-thirds full. Using a 50ml (1¾fl oz) ice-cream scoop can make this process easier and will result in even cupcakes.

6. Cut the coconut chocolate bars into 12–16 even pieces and place one piece into each unbaked cupcake. Bake for 20–25 minutes or until the sponge bounces back when lightly touched. Leave to cool slightly before removing from the tin and placing on a wire rack to cool completely before frosting.

7. Using a freestanding electric mixer with the paddle attachment or a hand-held electric whisk, gradually mix the icing sugar and butter together on a low speed until combined and there are no large lumps of butter. Add the coconut milk while mixing on a slow speed, then increase the speed and beat the frosting until light and fluffy.

8. Cut the remaining 1–2 coconut bars into pieces, one per cupcake Once the cupcakes are cool, spoon generous amounts of the frosting onto each cupcake, then gently smooth over with a palette knife, making a swirl at the top if you wish. Coat each cupcake in desiccated coconut and top with a piece of coconut chocolate.

Nothing beats accompanying a cup of tea with a custard cream; except, perhaps, our cupcake version of this well-loved classic biscuit! You can always bake and assemble the cookies the day before and store them in an airtight container, then finish the recipe the following day.

Custard Cream Cupcakes

MAKES 12–16 CUPCAKES

FOR THE COOKIES

100g (3½oz) UNSALTED BUTTER, SOFTENED

140g (5oz) CASTER SUGAR

1 EGG

200g (7oz) PLAIN FLOUR, PLUS EXTRA FOR DUSTING

¼ tsp CREAM OF TARTAR

FOR THE SPONGE

70g (2½oz) UNSALTED BUTTER, SOFTENED

210g (7½oz) PLAIN FLOUR

250g (9oz) CASTER SUGAR

1 tbsp BAKING POWDER

½ tsp SALT

210ml (7½fl oz) WHOLE MILK

2 LARGE EGGS

1 tsp VANILLA EXTRACT

FOR THE CUSTARD

220ml (8fl oz) WHOLE MILK

2 LARGE EGG YOLKS

1 tsp VANILLA EXTRACT

40g (1½oz) CASTER SUGAR

15g (½oz) PLAIN FLOUR

15g (½oz) CORNFLOUR

Ingredients continue …

1. First make the cookies. Preheat the oven to 170°C (325°F), Gas mark 3, and line a baking tray with baking parchment.

2. In a freestanding electric mixer with the paddle attachment or using a hand-held electric whisk, cream the butter and sugar until light and fluffy. Add the egg and mix until fully incorporated. In a small bowl, sift the flour and cream of tartar together. Add the dry ingredients to the butter and egg mixture. Mix on a slow speed until a dough forms. Don't overmix.

3. Roll out the dough on a lightly floured surface, to about 3–4mm (⅛in) thick. Using the cookie cutter, cut out 32 (or more) cookies. Carefully place them on the prepared baking tray. Bake the cookies for approximately 10–13 minutes or until they start to go golden brown around the edges. Set aside to cool completely for later use. Any excess dough can be made into more cookies or frozen and used again at a later stage.

4. Leave the oven turned to 170°C (325°F), Gas mark 3, and line the muffin tins with paper muffin cases to make the number of cupcakes you require.

5. In the freestanding electric mixer with the paddle attachment or using the hand-held electric whisk, mix the butter, flour, sugar, baking powder and salt together until they form a crumb-like consistency.

6. In a jug, mix together the milk, eggs and vanilla extract by hand.

7. With the mixer or whisk on a slow speed, gradually pour half of the liquid into the crumb mixture and mix thoroughly until combined. Raise the speed to medium and beat until the batter is smooth and thick with no lumps. Scrape down the sides of the bowl occasionally. Once all lumps have been beaten out, reduce the speed and gradually pour in the remaining liquid, continuing to mix until the batter is smooth and combined.

Recipe continues …

8. Spoon the batter into the prepared paper cases, filling them two-thirds full. Using a 50ml (1¾fl oz) ice-cream scoop can make this process easier and will result in even cupcakes. Bake for approximately 20–25 minutes or until golden brown and the sponge bounces back when lightly touched. Leave to cool slightly before removing from the tin and placing on a wire rack to cool completely before frosting.

9. While the cupcakes are baking, make the custard. Place the milk in a saucepan and bring to the boil. In a bowl, mix together the egg yolks, vanilla extract, sugar, flour and cornflour to make a paste, adding 1 tablespoon of the hot milk to thin if necessary.

10. When the milk has boiled, remove the pan from the heat and mix 4–5 tablespoons with the egg and flour paste, then pour this back into the pan with the remaining hot milk and return to the heat.

11. Bring back up to the boil, whisking constantly, and continue to boil for a further 3–4 minutes to ensure the flour and cornflour are fully cooked. However, be careful not to overcook or the eggs may begin to scramble. Remove from the heat and immediately pour the custard into a baking tray. Cover at once with cling film and set aside to cool completely.

12. Using the freestanding electric mixer with the paddle attachment or the hand-held electric whisk, make the frosting by gradually mixing the icing sugar and butter together on a low speed until combined and there are no large lumps of butter. Gradually pour in the milk and vanilla extract, while mixing on a slow speed. When all the liquid is incorporated, turn the mixer up to a high speed and beat the frosting until light and fluffy. Colour the frosting a very pale yellow using liquid food colouring, mixing it through until all of the frosting is the same shade.

13. To assemble the mini cookies for decoration, place a small amount of the prepared frosting in a piping bag. Lay out half the cooled cookies on a tray. Pipe a small amount of frosting onto each cookie, and then sandwich together with the remaining cookies.

14. Once the cupcakes are cool, use a sharp knife to make a hollow in the centre of each cupcake, approximately 2cm (¾in) in diameter and about 3cm (1¼in) deep. Retain the cut-out piece of sponge. Spoon about 1–2 teaspoons of the custard into the hollow and replace the cut-out piece of sponge, trimming to fit and pressing down gently to ensure that the top is level with the rest of the cake.

15. Spoon generous amounts of the frosting onto each cupcake, then gently smooth over with a palette knife, making a swirl at the top if you wish. Top each cupcake with a mini custard cream sandwich cookie.

Caramel, hazelnuts and chocolate are a delicious combination. These cupcakes take a little time to make but are perfect as a gift or for a celebration. You can make the praline up to two days in advance and store in an airtight container.

Praline Chocolate Cupcakes

MAKES 12–16 CUPCAKES

FOR THE SPONGE

70g (2½oz) UNSALTED BUTTER, SOFTENED

170g (6oz) PLAIN FLOUR

250g (9oz) CASTER SUGAR

50g (1¾oz) COCOA POWDER, SIFTED

1 tbsp BAKING POWDER

½ tsp SALT

210ml (7½fl oz) WHOLE MILK

2 LARGE EGGS

FOR THE FROSTING

450g (1lb) ICING SUGAR, SIFTED

60g (2oz) COCOA POWDER, SIFTED

150g (5½oz) UNSALTED BUTTER, SOFTENED

60ml (2fl oz) WHOLE MILK

FOR THE PRALINE

65g (2oz) CHOPPED HAZELNUTS

130g (4½oz) CASTER SUGAR

50ml (1¾fl oz) WATER

EQUIPMENT

ONE OR TWO 12-HOLE DEEP MUFFIN TINS

1. Preheat the oven to 170°C (325°F), Gas mark 3, and line the muffin tins with paper muffin cases to make the number you require.

2. First make the sponge. In a freestanding electric mixer with the paddle attachment or using a hand-held electric whisk, mix the butter, flour, sugar, cocoa powder, baking powder and salt together until they form a crumb-like consistency.

3. In a jug, mix together the milk and eggs by hand.

4. With the mixer or whisk on a slow speed, gradually pour half of the liquid into the crumb mixture and mix thoroughly until combined. Raise the speed to medium and mix until the batter is smooth and thick, with no lumps. Scrape down the sides of the bowl from time to time. Once all lumps are gone, turn the speed back down and gradually pour in the remaining liquid, continuing to mix until the batter is smooth and combined.

5. Spoon the batter into the prepared paper cases, filling them two-thirds full. Using a 50ml (1¾fl oz) ice-cream scoop can make this process easier and will result in even cupcakes.

6. Bake for 20–25 minutes or until the sponge bounces back when lightly touched. Leave to cool slightly before removing from the tin and placing on a wire rack to cool completely before frosting.

7. Using the freestanding electric mixer with the paddle attachment or the hand-held electric whisk, gradually mix the icing sugar, cocoa powder and butter together on a low speed until combined and there are no large lumps of butter. Gradually add the milk while mixing on a slow speed. Increase the speed and beat the frosting until light and fluffy.

Recipe continues …

8. For the praline, line a baking tray with baking parchment and spread the chopped hazelnuts evenly in the tray. Place the sugar and water in a medium saucepan and bring to the boil. Allow the mixture to bubble for about 15 minutes until it forms a golden caramel. Do not stir while the mixture is boiling or the caramel will crystallise; just gently swirl the pan from time to time.

9. Once the caramel is ready, carefully pour it over the chopped nuts, making sure all the nuts are covered. Allow this to cool and set completely. Once cold and set, break up the praline into small chunks, then use a food processor to chop up the praline into fine pieces. (This praline needs to be stored in an airtight container if not using straight away.)

10. Once the cupcakes are cool, spoon generous amounts of the frosting onto each cupcake, then gently smooth over with a palette knife, making a swirl at the top if you wish. Sprinkle each cupcake with a generous amount of praline.

The rose-flavoured custard in these cakes is irresistible. You can find rose water in larger supermarkets, Middle Eastern food shops or online.

Rose Chocolate Cupcakes

MAKES 12–16 CUPCAKES

FOR THE SPONGE

70g (2½oz) UNSALTED BUTTER, SOFTENED

170g (6oz) PLAIN FLOUR

250g (9oz) CASTER SUGAR

50g (1¾oz) COCOA POWDER, SIFTED

1 tbsp BAKING POWDER

½ tsp SALT

210ml (7½fl oz) WHOLE MILK

2 LARGE EGGS

2 tbsp ROSE WATER

FOR THE CUSTARD

330ml (11½fl oz) WHOLE MILK

1 tbsp ROSE WATER

3 LARGE EGG YOLKS

60g (2oz) CASTER SUGAR

20g (¾oz) PLAIN FLOUR

20g (¾oz) CORNFLOUR

Ingredients continue ...

1. Preheat the oven to 170°C (325°F), Gas mark 3, and line the muffin tins with paper muffin cases to make the number you require.

2. First make the sponge. In a freestanding electric mixer with the paddle attachment or using a hand-held electric whisk, mix the butter, flour, sugar, cocoa powder, baking powder and salt together until they form a crumb-like consistency.

3. In a jug, mix together the milk, eggs and rose water by hand.

4. With the mixer or whisk on a slow speed, gradually pour half of the liquid into the crumb mixture and mix thoroughly until combined. Raise the speed to medium and beat until the batter is smooth and thick, with no lumps. Scrape down the sides of the bowl now and then. Once all lumps are gone, turn the speed back down and gradually pour in the remaining liquid, continuing to mix until the batter is smooth and combined.

5. Spoon the batter into the prepared paper cases, filling them two-thirds full. Using a 50ml (1¾fl oz) ice-cream scoop can make this process easier and will result in even cupcakes.

6. Bake for 20–25 minutes or until the sponge bounces back when lightly touched. Leave to cool slightly before removing from the tin and placing on a wire rack to cool completely before frosting.

7. While the cupcakes are baking, make the custard for the filling. Place the milk and rose water in a saucepan and bring to the boil. In a bowl, mix together the egg yolks, sugar, flour and cornflour to make a paste, adding 1 tablespoon of the hot milk to thin if necessary.

8. When the milk has boiled, remove the pan from the heat and mix 4–5 tablespoons with the egg and flour paste, then pour this back into the pan with the remaining hot milk and return to the heat.

Recipe continues ...

FOR THE FROSTING

450g (1lb) ICING SUGAR, SIFTED

60g (2oz) COCOA POWDER, SIFTED

150g (5½oz) UNSALTED BUTTER, SOFTENED

60ml (2fl oz) WHOLE MILK

2 tbsp ROSE WATER

FOR THE DECORATION

SLICED PINK TURKISH DELIGHT

EQUIPMENT

ONE OR TWO 12-HOLE DEEP MUFFIN TINS

9. Bring back up to the boil, whisking constantly, and continue to boil for a further 3–4 minutes to ensure the flour and cornflour are fully cooked. However, be careful not to overcook or the eggs may begin to scramble. Remove from the heat and immediately pour the custard into a baking tray. Cover directly with cling film and set aside to cool completely.

10. Using the freestanding electric mixer with the paddle attachment or the hand-held electric whisk, gradually mix the icing sugar, cocoa powder and butter together on a low speed until combined and there are no large lumps of butter. Then gradually add the milk and rose water while mixing on a slow speed. Once incorporated, turn up the speed and beat the frosting until light and fluffy.

11. Once the cupcakes are cool, use a sharp knife to make a hollow in the centre of each cupcake, approximately 2cm (¾in) in diameter and about 3cm (1¼in) deep. Retain the cut-out piece of sponge. Spoon about 1–2 teaspoons of the rose custard into each hollow.

12. Replace the cut-out piece of sponge, trimming to fit and pressing down gently to ensure that the top is level with the rest of the cake. Spoon generous amounts of the frosting onto each cupcake, then gently smooth over with a palette knife, making a swirl at the top if you wish.

13. Top each cupcake with thin slices of pink Turkish delight.

These cupcakes will wow your friends and colleagues. Making your own toffee isn't hard but you need to be patient and remember not to stir the caramel as it boils. Investing in a sugar thermometer is worthwhile and will help you ensure that the toffee comes up to the correct temperature as it boils, which is important to achieve the delicious cinder flavour.

Cinder Toffee Cupcakes

MAKES 12–16 CUPCAKES

FOR THE SPONGE

70g (2½oz) UNSALTED BUTTER, SOFTENED

170g (6oz) PLAIN FLOUR

250g (9oz) CASTER SUGAR

50g (1¾oz) COCOA POWDER, SIFTED

1 tbsp BAKING POWDER

½ tsp SALT

210ml (7½fl oz) WHOLE MILK

2 LARGE EGGS

FOR THE CINDER TOFFEE

75g (2½oz) GOLDEN SYRUP

170g (6oz) CASTER SUGAR

30ml (1fl oz) WATER

1 tsp BICARBONATE OF SODA

FOR THE FROSTING

450g (1lb) ICING SUGAR, SIFTED

60g (2oz) COCOA POWDER, SIFTED

160g (5½oz) UNSALTED BUTTER, SOFTENED

60ml (2fl oz) WHOLE MILK

EQUIPMENT

ONE OR TWO 12-HOLE DEEP MUFFIN TINS

SUGAR THERMOMETER

1. Preheat the oven to 170°C (325°F), Gas mark 3, and line the muffin tins with paper muffin cases to make the number you require.

2. First make the sponge. In a freestanding electric mixer with the paddle attachment or using a hand-held electric whisk, mix the butter, flour, sugar, cocoa powder, baking powder and salt together until they form a crumb-like consistency.

3. In a jug, mix together the milk and eggs by hand.

4. With the mixer or whisk on a slow speed, gradually pour half of the liquid into the crumb mixture and mix thoroughly until combined. Raise the speed to medium and mix until the batter is smooth and thick, with no lumps. Scrape down the sides of the bowl from time to time. Once any lumps are gone, turn the speed back down and gradually pour in the remaining liquid, continuing to mix until the batter is smooth and combined.

5. Spoon the batter into the prepared paper cases, filling them two-thirds full. Using a 50ml (1¾fl oz) ice-cream scoop can make this process easier and will result in even cupcakes.

6. Bake for 20–25 minutes or until the sponge bounces back when lightly touched. Leave to cool slightly before removing from the tin and placing on a wire rack to cool completely before frosting.

7. Meanwhile, make the cinder toffee. Line a baking tray with baking parchment, making sure the paper lines the base and sides of the tray. In a large, high-sided saucepan, mix the golden syrup, caster sugar and water together and bring to the boil. Boil until it reaches the hard crack stage (when a drop of boiling syrup immersed in cold water cracks) — about 150°C (302°F) on a sugar thermometer. Do not stir while the mixture is boiling or the caramel will crystallise; just gently swirl the pan from time to time.

Recipe continues …

8. When the mixture reaches the right temperature, whisk in the bicarbonate of soda – the mixture will froth up quite vigorously. Wearing oven gloves, carefully pour the toffee immediately into the prepared tray. Leave to cool and set completely.

9. Using a freestanding electric mixer with the paddle attachment or a hand-held electric whisk, gradually mix the icing sugar, cocoa powder and butter together on a low speed until combined and there are no large lumps of butter. Gradually add the milk while mixing on a slow speed. Once incorporated, increase the speed and beat until light and fluffy.

10. Break up the cinder toffee into small, rough pieces using a rolling pin. Mix the cinder toffee pieces into the frosting by hand, reserving some for decoration.

11. Once the cupcakes are cool, spoon generous amounts of the frosting onto each cupcake, then gently smooth over with a palette knife, making a swirl at the top if you wish. Top each cupcake with the remaining crushed cinder toffee.

We wanted to take our popular Grasshopper Pie and turn it into a cupcake and here is the result. These are one of the most popular daily specials we sell, a real American treat! Use good-quality peppermint extract or essence rather than an artificial flavouring for the best-tasting results.

Grasshopper Cupcakes

MAKES 12-16 CUPCAKES

FOR THE SPONGE
70g (2½oz) UNSALTED BUTTER, SOFTENED
170g (6oz) PLAIN FLOUR
250g (9oz) CASTER SUGAR
50g (1¾oz) COCOA POWDER, SIFTED
1 tbsp BAKING POWDER
½ tsp SALT
210ml (7½fl oz) WHOLE MILK
2 LARGE EGGS

FOR THE FILLING
60ml (2fl oz) DOUBLE CREAM
60g (2oz) WHITE CHOCOLATE CHIPS
1ml (drop) PEPPERMINT ESSENCE
1ml (drop) GREEN LIQUID FOOD COLOURING

FOR THE CUSTARD
330ml (11½fl oz) WHOLE MILK
3 LARGE EGG YOLKS
60g (2oz) CASTER SUGAR
20g (¾oz) PLAIN FLOUR
20g (¾oz) CORNFLOUR
150ml (5½fl oz) DOUBLE CREAM

FOR THE DECORATION
60g (2oz) CHOCOLATE COOKIES

EQUIPMENT
ONE OR TWO 12-HOLE DEEP MUFFIN TINS

1. Preheat the oven to 170°C (325°F), Gas mark 3, and line the muffin tins with paper muffin cases to make the number you require.

2. First make the sponge. In a freestanding electric mixer with the paddle attachment or using a hand-held electric whisk, mix the butter, flour, sugar, cocoa powder, baking powder and salt together until they form a crumb-like consistency.

3. In a jug, mix together the milk and eggs by hand.

4. With the mixer or whisk on a slow speed, slowly pour half of the liquid into the crumb mixture and mix thoroughly until combined. Turn up the speed to medium and mix until the batter is smooth and thick with no lumps. Scrape down the sides of the bowl from time to time. Once the mixture is smooth, reduce the speed and gradually pour in the remaining liquid from the jug, continuing to mix until the batter is smooth and combined once more.

5. Spoon the batter into the prepared paper cases, filling them two-thirds full. Using a 50ml (1¾fl oz) ice-cream scoop can make this process easier and will result in even cupcakes.

6. Bake for approximately 20–25 minutes or until the sponge bounces back when lightly touched. Leave to cool slightly before removing from the tin and placing on a wire rack to cool completely before frosting.

7. While the cakes are baking, make the mint filling. Heat up the double cream in a jug in the microwave, or on the stove in a very small pan, until almost boiling. Place the white chocolate chips in a medium bowl. Pour the hot cream over the white chocolate. Let this sit for a couple of minutes to allow the chocolate to start to melt. Then stir in the peppermint essence and green food colouring and keep stirring until all the chocolate has melted and the mixture is smooth. Place in the fridge to set. Once set, whip up the filling by hand. (Please be careful when whipping this up as it will split if over-whipped.)

Recipe continues ...

8. To make the custard for the frosting, place the milk in a saucepan and bring to the boil. In a bowl, mix together the egg yolks, sugar, flour and cornflour to make a paste, adding 1 tablespoon of the hot milk to thin if necessary.

9. When the milk has boiled, remove the pan from the heat and mix 4–5 tablespoons with the egg and flour paste, then pour this back into the pan with the remaining hot milk and return to the heat.

10. Bring back up to the boil, whisking constantly, and continue to boil for a further 3–4 minutes to ensure the flour and cornflour are fully cooked. However, be careful not to overcook or the eggs may begin to scramble. Remove from the heat and immediately pour the custard into a baking tray. Cover at once with cling film and set aside to cool completely.

11. In a food processor, blend the whole chocolate cookies (and filling, if they have one) until they form fine crumbs.

12. To finish the custard, pour the double cream into a medium bowl. Using a freestanding electric mixer with the whisk attachment or a hand-held electric whisk, beat the cream until it forms soft peaks. Place the cooled custard into a medium bowl. With the mixer or whisk on a slow speed, mix the custard until it is smooth. Using a spatula, gradually fold the whipped cream into the custard.

13. Once the cupcakes are cool, use a sharp knife to make a hollow in the centre of each cupcake, approximately 2cm (¾in) in diameter and about 3cm (1¼in) deep. Retain the cut-out piece of sponge. Spoon about 1–2 teaspoons of the mint filling into the hollow. Replace the cut-out piece of sponge, trimming to fit and pressing down gently to ensure that the top is level with the rest of the cake.

14. Spoon generous amounts of the custard onto each cupcake, then gently smooth over with a palette knife, making a swirl at the top if you wish. Top each cupcake with a sprinkling of the chocolate cookie crumbs.

This quintessentially British pudding turned into a cupcake is part of our popular summer desserts range. Make sure you eat these soon after decorating so that the meringue stays crisp on top.

Eton Mess Cupcakes

MAKES 12–16 CUPCAKES

FOR THE SPONGE

70g (2½oz) UNSALTED BUTTER, SOFTENED

210g (7½oz) PLAIN FLOUR

250g (9oz) CASTER SUGAR

1 tbsp BAKING POWDER

½ tsp SALT

210ml (7½fl oz) WHOLE MILK

2 LARGE EGGS

1 tsp VANILLA EXTRACT

FOR THE CUSTARD

330ml (11½oz) WHOLE MILK

3 LARGE EGG YOLKS

60g (2oz) CASTER SUGAR

20g (¾oz) PLAIN FLOUR

20g (¾oz) CORNFLOUR

150ml (5½fl oz) DOUBLE CREAM

FOR THE DECORATION

125g (4½oz) STRAWBERRIES, CUT INTO ROUGH PIECES

50g (1¾oz) SHOP-BOUGHT OR READY-MADE MERINGUE, CRUSHED INTO ROUGH PIECES

EQUIPMENT

ONE OR TWO 12-HOLE DEEP MUFFIN TINS

1. Preheat the oven to 170°C (325°F), Gas mark 3, and line the muffin tins with paper muffin cases to make the number you require.

2. First make the sponge. In a freestanding electric mixer with the paddle attachment or using a hand-held electric whisk, mix the butter, flour, sugar, baking powder and salt together until they form a crumb-like consistency.

3. In a separate jug, mix together the milk, eggs and vanilla extract by hand.

4. With the mixer or whisk on a slow speed, slowly pour half of the liquid into the crumb mixture and mix thoroughly until combined. Turn up the speed to medium and beat the batter until smooth and thick with no lumps. Scrape down the sides of the bowl as you go. Once any lumps have been beaten out, reduce the speed and gradually add the remaining liquid from the jug, continuing to mix until the batter is smooth and combined once more.

5. Spoon the batter into the prepared paper cases, filling them two-thirds full. Using a 50ml (1¾fl oz) ice-cream scoop can make this process easier and will result in even cupcakes.

6. Bake for approximately 20–25 minutes or until golden brown and the sponge bounces back when lightly touched. Leave to cool slightly before removing from the tin and placing on a wire rack to cool completely before frosting.

7. While the cupcakes are baking, make the custard for the topping. Place the milk in a saucepan and bring to the boil. In a bowl, mix together the egg yolks, sugar, flour and cornflour to make a paste, adding 1 tablespoon of the hot milk to thin if necessary.

Recipe continues …

8. When the milk has boiled, remove the pan from the heat and mix 4–5 tablespoons with the egg and flour paste, then pour this back into the pan with the remaining hot milk and return to the heat. Bring back up to the boil, whisking constantly, and continue to boil for a further 3–4 minutes to ensure the flour and cornflour are fully cooked. However, be careful not to overcook or the eggs may begin to scramble. Remove from the heat and immediately pour the custard into a baking tray. Cover directly with cling film and set aside to cool completely.

9. To finish the custard, pour the double cream into a medium bowl. Using the freestanding electric mixer with the whisk attachment or the hand-held electric whisk, beat the cream until it forms soft peaks. Place the cooled custard into a medium bowl. With the mixer or whisk on a slow speed, mix the custard until it is smooth. Using a spatula, gradually fold the whipped cream into the custard.

10. Once the cupcakes are cool, use a sharp knife to make a hollow in the centre of each cupcake, approximately 2cm (¾in) in diameter and about 3cm (1¼in) deep. Retain the cut-out piece of sponge. Spoon about 1 teaspoon of the chopped strawberries into the hollow. Replace the cut-out piece of sponge, trimming to fit and pressing down gently to ensure that the top is level with the rest of the cake.

11. Spoon generous amounts of the custard onto each cupcake, then gently smooth over with a palette knife, making a swirl at the top if you wish. Top each cupcake with some chopped strawberry pieces and a generous sprinkling of crushed meringue.

A classic French dessert given the American cupcake treatment. Sprinkle a generous amount of demerara sugar over the custard before 'burning' the sugar to create the classic crunchy brûlée topping. This recipe requires a cook's blowtorch — make sure you read the instructions and do be careful if you've not used one before.

Crème Brûlée Cupcakes

MAKES 12–16 CUPCAKES

FOR THE CUSTARD
330ml (11½ fl oz) WHOLE MILK
3 LARGE EGG YOLKS
60g (2oz) CASTER SUGAR
20g (¾oz) PLAIN FLOUR
20g (¾oz) CORNFLOUR

FOR THE SPONGE
70g (2½oz) UNSALTED BUTTER, SOFTENED
210g (7½oz) PLAIN FLOUR
250g (9oz) CASTER SUGAR
1 tbsp BAKING POWDER
½ tsp SALT
210ml (7½ fl oz) WHOLE MILK
2 LARGE EGGS
1 tsp VANILLA EXTRACT

FOR THE DECORATION
150g (5½oz) DEMERARA SUGAR

EQUIPMENT
ONE OR TWO 12-HOLE DEEP MUFFIN TINS
COOK'S BLOWTORCH

1. To make the custard, place the milk in a saucepan and bring to the boil. In a bowl, mix together the egg yolks, sugar, flour and cornflour to make a paste, adding 1 tablespoon of the hot milk to thin if necessary.

2. When the milk has boiled, remove the pan from the heat and mix 4–5 tablespoons with the egg and flour paste, then pour this back into the pan with the remaining hot milk and return to the heat.

3. Bring back up to the boil, whisking constantly, and continue to boil for a further 3–4 minutes to ensure the flour and cornflour are fully cooked. However, be careful not to overcook or the eggs may begin to scramble. Remove from the heat and immediately pour the custard into a baking tray. Cover directly with cling film and set aside to cool completely.

4. Meanwhile, make the sponge. Preheat the oven to 170°C (325°F), Gas mark 3, and line the muffin tins with paper muffin cases to make the number you require.

5. In a freestanding electric mixer with the paddle attachment or using a hand-held electric whisk, mix the butter, flour, sugar, baking powder and salt together until they form a crumb-like consistency.

6. In a jug, mix together the milk, eggs and vanilla extract by hand.

7. With the mixer or whisk on a slow speed, gradually pour half of the liquid into the crumb mixture and mix thoroughly until combined. Turn up the speed to medium and beat until the batter is smooth and thick with no lumps. Scrape down the sides of the bowl from time to time. Once any lumps have been beaten out, reduce the speed and gradually pour in the remaining liquid, continuing to mix until the batter is smooth and combined.

Recipe continues …

8. Spoon the batter into the prepared paper cases, filling them two-thirds full. Using a 50ml (1¾fl oz) ice-cream scoop can make this process easier and will result in even cupcakes.

9. Bake for approximately 20–25 minutes or until the cupcakes are golden brown and the sponge bounces back when lightly touched. Leave to cool slightly before removing from the tin and placing on a wire rack to cool completely before frosting.

10. In the freestanding electric mixer with the paddle attachment or using the hand-held electric whisk on a slow speed, mix the custard until it is smooth. Spoon generous amounts of the custard onto each cupcake, then gently smooth over with a palette knife, making a swirl at the top if you wish.

11. Coat the top of each cupcake generously in demerara sugar. Using a cook's blowtorch, carefully brûlée (lightly burn) the sugar, avoiding the paper cases with the flame. These cupcakes should be served immediately.

The stem ginger in these cupcakes gives a mouthwateringly sweet and strong flavour without the peppery taste of fresh ginger. Crystallised ginger can be found in the baking section of most large supermarkets.

Ginger Chocolate Cupcakes

MAKES 12-16 CUPCAKES

FOR THE SPONGE

70g (2½oz) UNSALTED BUTTER, SOFTENED

170g (6oz) PLAIN FLOUR

250g (9oz) CASTER SUGAR

50g (1¾oz) COCOA POWDER

1 tbsp BAKING POWDER

1 tsp GROUND GINGER

½ tsp SALT

210ml (7½fl oz) WHOLE MILK

2 LARGE EGGS

3 tbsp FINELY CHOPPED STEM GINGER (ABOUT 3 BALLS)

FOR THE FROSTING

450g (1lb) ICING SUGAR, SIFTED

60g (2oz) COCOA POWDER, SIFTED

150g (5½oz) UNSALTED BUTTER, SOFTENED

3 tbsp FINELY CHOPPED STEM GINGER (ABOUT 3 BALLS)

60ml (2fl oz) WHOLE MILK

FOR THE DECORATION

CRYSTALLISED GINGER

EQUIPMENT

ONE OR TWO 12-HOLE DEEP MUFFIN TINS

1. Preheat the oven to 170°C (325°F), Gas mark 3, and line the muffin tins with paper muffin cases to make the number you require.

2. First make the sponge. In a freestanding electric mixer with the paddle attachment or using a hand-held electric whisk, mix the butter, flour, sugar, cocoa powder, baking powder, ground ginger and salt together until they form a crumb-like consistency.

3. In a jug, mix together the milk and eggs by hand.

4. With the mixer or whisk on a slow speed, gradually pour half of the liquid into the crumb mixture and mix thoroughly until combined. Raise the speed to medium and mix until the batter is smooth and thick, with no lumps. Scrape down the sides of the bowl occasionally. Once all lumps are gone, turn the speed back down and gradually pour in the remaining liquid, continuing to mix until the batter is smooth and combined. Mix through the chopped stem ginger.

5. Spoon the batter into the prepared paper cases, filling them two-thirds full. Using a 50ml (1¾fl oz) ice-cream scoop can make this process easier and will result in even cupcakes.

6. Bake for 20–25 minutes or until the cupcakes bounce back when lightly touched. Leave to cool slightly before removing from the tin and placing on a wire rack to cool completely before frosting.

7. Using a freestanding electric mixer with the paddle attachment or a hand-held electric whisk, gradually mix the icing sugar, cocoa powder and butter together on a low speed until combined and there are no large lumps of butter. Then mix through the chopped stem ginger. Gradually add the milk while mixing on a slow speed. Once incorporated, increase the speed and beat until light and fluffy.

8. When the cupcakes are cool, spoon a generous amount of the frosting onto each cupcake, then gently smooth over with a palette knife, making a swirl at the top if you wish. Top each cupcake with a couple of pieces of crystallised ginger.

A tangy classic American pie given our special Hummingbird cupcake treatment. We don't use colouring in the custard frosting, so it does come out pale. Grate over lots of lime zest to decorate and add a bit of zing.

Key Lime Cupcakes

MAKES 12–16 CUPCAKES

FOR THE LIME CURD

2 LARGE EGGS

50g (1¾oz) UNSALTED BUTTER

225g (8oz) CASTER SUGAR

GRATED ZEST and JUICE OF 2 LIMES

50ml (1¾fl oz) DOUBLE CREAM

FOR THE SPONGE

70g (2½oz) UNSALTED BUTTER, SOFTENED

210g (7½oz) PLAIN FLOUR

250g (9oz) CASTER SUGAR

1 tbsp BAKING POWDER

½ tsp SALT

210ml (7½fl oz) WHOLE MILK

2 LARGE EGGS

1 tsp VANILLA EXTRACT

FOR THE CUSTARD

330ml (11½fl oz) WHOLE MILK

3 LARGE EGG YOLKS

60g (2oz) CASTER SUGAR

20g (¾oz) PLAIN FLOUR

20g (¾oz) CORNFLOUR

150ml (5½fl oz) DOUBLE CREAM

Ingredients continue ...

1. First make the lime curd. In a medium pan, gently heat the eggs, butter, caster sugar and lime juice, whisking continuously until thick. Strain the thick mixture into a large mixing bowl and stir in the lime zest. Cover directly with cling film (so that it is touching the surface of the curd) and set aside to cool completely.

2. Using a freestanding electric mixer with the whisk attachment or a hand-held electric whisk, beat the cream until it forms soft peaks. Fold the double cream into the cooled lime curd.

3. Preheat the oven to 170°C (325°F), Gas mark 3, and line the muffin tins with paper muffin cases to make the number you require.

4. In a freestanding electric mixer with the paddle attachment or using a hand-held electric whisk, mix the butter, flour, sugar, baking powder and salt together until they form a crumb-like consistency.

5. In a separate jug, mix together the milk, eggs and vanilla extract by hand.

6. With the mixer or whisk on a slow speed, gradually pour half of the liquid into the crumb mixture and mix thoroughly until combined. Turn up the speed and beat until the batter is smooth and thick with no lumps. Scrape down the sides of the bowl as needed. Reduce the speed again and gradually add the rest of the liquid from the jug, continuing to mix until the batter is smooth and combined.

7. Spoon the batter into the prepared paper cases, filling them two-thirds full. Using a 50ml (1¾fl oz) ice-cream scoop can make this process easier and will result in even cupcakes.

8. Bake for approximately 20–25 minutes or until golden brown and the sponge bounces back when lightly touched. Leave to cool slightly before removing from the tin and placing on a wire rack to cool completely before frosting.

Recipe continues ...

9. While the cupcakes are cooking, make the custard for the topping. Place the milk in a saucepan and bring to the boil. In a bowl, mix together the egg yolks, sugar, flour and cornflour to make a paste, adding 1 tablespoon of the hot milk to thin it if necessary.

10. When the milk has boiled, remove the pan from the heat and mix 4–5 tablespoons with the egg and flour paste, then pour this back into the pan with the remaining hot milk and return to the heat.

11. Bring back up to the boil, whisking constantly, and continue to boil for a further 3–4 minutes to ensure the flour and cornflour are fully cooked. However, be careful not to overcook or the eggs may begin to scramble. Remove from the heat and immediately pour the custard into a baking tray. Cover directly with cling film and set aside to cool completely.

12. Once the cupcakes are cool, use a sharp knife to make a hollow in the centre of each cupcake, approximately 2cm (¾in) in diameter and about 3cm (1¼in) deep. Retain the cut-out piece of sponge. Spoon about 1–2 teaspoons of the creamy lime curd into the hollow. Replace the cut-out piece of sponge, trimming to fit and pressing down gently to ensure that the top is level with the rest of the cake.

13. To finish the custard, pour the double cream into a medium bowl. Using a freestanding electric mixer with the whisk attachment or a hand-held electric whisk, beat the cream until it forms soft peaks. Place the cooled custard into a medium bowl. With the mixer or whisk on a slow speed, mix the custard until it is smooth. Using a spatula, gradually fold the whipped cream into the custard.

14. Spoon generous amounts of the custard onto each cupcake, then gently smooth over with a palette knife, making a swirl at the top if you wish. Top each cupcake with a sprinkling of lime zest and digestive biscuit crumbs.

We first tried this recipe with home-made custard, but it didn't quite capture the quintessentially British flavour combination of the popular boiled sweets, so we used custard powder instead. You can use fresh, tinned or frozen rhubarb for a fantastic result.

Rhubarb & Custard Cupcakes

MAKES 12–16 CUPCAKES

FOR THE RHUBARB FILLING
120g (4oz) RHUBARB, CUT INTO SMALL PIECES
50g (1¾oz) UNSALTED BUTTER
120g (4oz) CASTER SUGAR
RED LIQUID FOOD COLOURING

FOR THE SPONGE
70g (2½oz) UNSALTED BUTTER, SOFTENED
210g (7½oz) PLAIN FLOUR
250g (9oz) CASTER SUGAR
1 tbsp BAKING POWDER
½ tsp SALT
210ml (7½fl oz) WHOLE MILK
2 LARGE EGGS
1 tsp VANILLA EXTRACT

FOR THE CUSTARD
70g (2½oz) CUSTARD POWDER
35g (1¼oz) CASTER SUGAR
600ml (1 pint) WHOLE MILK
1 tsp VANILLA EXTRACT
RED LIQUID FOOD COLOURING

EQUIPMENT
ONE OR TWO 12-HOLE DEEP MUFFIN TINS

1. To make the rhubarb filling, in a medium pan cook the rhubarb pieces, butter, caster sugar and a couple of tablespoons of water together. Cook on a medium heat until the rhubarb has completely broken up and is soft and cooked through — for approximately 15–20 minutes.

2. Take the pan off the heat and carefully add the red food colouring, a drop at a time, until the rhubarb is a light natural pink colour. Allow to cool completely. This can be made ahead and kept for up to 2 days.

3. Preheat the oven to 170°C (325°F), Gas mark 3, and line the muffin tins with paper muffin cases to make the number you require.

4. In a freestanding electric mixer with the paddle attachment or using a hand-held electric whisk, mix the butter, flour, sugar, baking powder and salt together until they form a crumb-like consistency.

5. In a separate jug, mix together the milk, eggs and vanilla extract by hand.

6. With the mixer or whisk on a slow speed, gradually pour half of the liquid into the crumb mixture and mix thoroughly until combined. Turn up the speed to medium and beat the batter until it is smooth and thick with no lumps. Scrape down the sides of the bowl as you go. Once any remaining lumps have gone, reduce the speed and gradually add the rest of the liquid from the jug, continuing to mix until the batter is smooth and combined.

7. Spoon the batter into the prepared paper cases, filling them two-thirds full. Using a 50ml (1¾fl oz) ice-cream scoop can make this process easier and will result in even cupcakes.

8. Bake for approximately 20–25 minutes or until the sponge bounces back when lightly touched. Leave to cool slightly before removing from the tin and placing on a wire rack to cool completely before frosting.

Recipe continues ...

9. While the cupcakes are baking, make the custard. Mix the custard powder and caster sugar together in a medium bowl and mix into a smooth paste with a little of the milk. Pour the remaining milk and the vanilla extract into a medium saucepan and bring to the boil.

10. Once the milk is boiling, pour a small amount into the custard powder paste. Off the heat, mix all of the custard paste mixture into the milk and stir well until it is fully incorporated.

11. Put the pan back onto the stove and allow the mixture to come back to the boil, whisking constantly to prevent lumps while thickening. The custard must thicken, come to the boil and cook for 15–20 minutes to cook the custard powder properly.

12. Once the custard is cooked, pour it onto a baking tray and cover directly with cling film. Set aside to cool completely.

13. When the cupcakes are cool, use a sharp knife to make a hollow in the centre of each cupcake, approximately 2cm (¾in) in diameter and about 3cm (1¼in) deep. Retain the cut-out piece of sponge. Spoon 1–2 teaspoons of the rhubarb filling into the hollow. Replace the cut-out piece of sponge, trimming to fit and pressing down gently to ensure that the top is level with the rest of the cake.

14. Divide the cooled custard into two equal parts. Colour one part a subtle pink using the red food colouring. To frost the cupcakes with the two custards, place a small dollop of yellow custard on one half of each cupcake and a small dollop of pink custard on the other half, then gently smooth over with a palette knife to produce a swirled two-tone appearance, finishing with a swirl at the top if you wish.

Toffee popcorn works best in this recipe. It's easiest to use shop-bought toffee popcorn (try not to eat it all before the cupcakes have even come out of the oven!) but if you want to make your own you can find some simple recipes online.

Popcorn Cupcakes

MAKES 12–16 CUPCAKES

FOR THE SPONGE
70g (2½oz) UNSALTED BUTTER, SOFTENED
210g (7½oz) PLAIN FLOUR
250g (9oz) CASTER SUGAR
1 tbsp BAKING POWDER
½ tsp SALT
210ml (7½fl oz) WHOLE MILK
2 LARGE EGGS
80g (3oz) TOFFEE POPCORN

FOR THE FROSTING
500g (1lb 2oz) ICING SUGAR, SIFTED
160g (5½oz) UNSALTED BUTTER, SOFTENED
50ml (1¾fl oz) WHOLE MILK
60g (2oz) TOFFEE POPCORN, CHOPPED

FOR THE DECORATION
50g (1¾oz) TOFFEE POPCORN
(3 PIECES OF POPCORN PER CUPCAKE)

EQUIPMENT
ONE OR TWO 12-HOLE DEEP MUFFIN TINS

1. Preheat the oven to 170°C (325°F), Gas mark 3, and line the muffin tins with paper muffin cases to make the number you require.

2. First make the sponge. In a freestanding electric mixer with the paddle attachment or using a hand-held electric whisk, mix the butter, flour, sugar, baking powder and salt together until they form a crumb-like consistency.

3. In a jug, mix together the milk and eggs by hand.

4. With the mixer or whisk on a slow speed, gradually pour half of the liquid into the crumb mixture and mix thoroughly until combined. Raise the speed to medium and mix until the batter is smooth and thick, with no lumps. Scrape down the sides of the bowl now and then. Once all lumps are gone, turn the speed back down and gradually pour in the remaining liquid, continuing to mix until the batter is smooth and combined.

5. Spoon the batter into the prepared paper cases, filling them two-thirds full. Using a 50ml (1¾fl oz) ice-cream scoop can make this process easier and will result in even cupcakes. Place four pieces of popcorn onto each unbaked cupcake. These will bake into the sponge.

6. Bake for 20–25 minutes or until the sponge bounces back when lightly touched. Leave to cool slightly before removing from the tin and placing on a wire rack to cool completely before frosting.

7. Using the freestanding electric mixer with the paddle attachment or the hand-held electric whisk, gradually mix the icing sugar and butter together on a low speed until combined and there are no large lumps of butter. Gradually pour in the milk, while mixing on a slow speed. When all the liquid is incorporated, turn the mixer up to a high speed and beat the frosting until light and fluffy.

8. Stir the chopped popcorn through the frosting, mixing well until evenly incorporated. Spoon generous amounts of the frosting onto each cupcake, then gently smooth over with a palette knife, making a swirl at the top if you wish. These cupcakes will have a rougher-textured appearance than others. Top each cupcake with three pieces of popcorn and serve immediately.

Liquorice is often a love-it or hate-it flavour. However, using liquorice-flavoured tea bags makes sure that the liquorice taste of these cupcakes is very subtle, so even people who don't usually like their allsorts will love these cakes.

Liquorice & Blackcurrant Cupcakes

MAKES 12–16 CUPCAKES

FOR THE SPONGE

4 LIQUORICE TEA BAGS

210ml (7½fl oz) WHOLE MILK

70g (2½oz) UNSALTED BUTTER, SOFTENED

210g (7½oz) PLAIN FLOUR

250g (9oz) CASTER SUGAR

1 tbsp BAKING POWDER

½ tsp SALT

2 LARGE EGGS

100g (3½oz) BLACKCURRANT JAM

FOR THE FROSTING

500g (1lb 2oz) ICING SUGAR, SIFTED

160g (5½oz) UNSALTED BUTTER, SOFTENED

50ml (1¾fl oz) WHOLE MILK

20ml (¾fl oz) BLACKCURRANT SYRUP/CORDIAL

FOR THE DECORATION

LIQUORICE SWEETS

EQUIPMENT

ONE OR TWO 12-HOLE DEEP MUFFIN TINS

1. In a jug, soak the liquorice tea bags in the milk for a couple of hours.

2. Preheat the oven to 170°C (325°F), Gas mark 3, and line the muffin tins with paper muffin cases to make the number you require.

3. In a freestanding electric mixer with the paddle attachment or using a hand-held electric whisk, mix the butter, flour, sugar, baking powder and salt together until they form a crumb-like consistency.

4. Squeeze the tea bags in the milk to get all the flavour out. Remove the tea bags from the milk and throw the bags away. Add the eggs to the jug of milk and mix together by hand.

5. With the mixer or whisk on a slow speed, gradually pour half the liquid into the crumb mixture and mix thoroughly until combined. Raise the speed to medium and beat the batter until it is smooth and thick with no lumps. Scrape down the sides of the bowl as you go. Once all lumps have been beaten out, reduce the speed and gradually pour in the rest of the liquid from the jug, continuing to mix the batter until smooth and combined.

6. Spoon the batter into the prepared paper cases, filling them two-thirds full. Using a 50ml (1¾fl oz) ice-cream scoop can make this process easier and will result in even cupcakes.

7. Bake for approximately 20–25 minutes or until the sponge bounces back when lightly touched. Leave to cool slightly before removing from the tin and placing on a wire rack to cool completely before frosting.

8. Using the freestanding electric mixer with the paddle attachment or the hand-held electric whisk, make the frosting by gradually mixing the icing sugar and butter together on a low speed until combined and there are no large lumps of butter.

Recipe continues ...

9. In a jug, mix the milk and blackcurrant syrup/cordial together. Gradually pour the milk into the butter and icing sugar while mixing on a slow speed. When all the liquid is incorporated, turn the mixer up to a high speed and beat the frosting until light and fluffy.

10. Once the cupcakes are cool, use a sharp knife to make a hollow in the centre of each cupcake, approximately 2cm (¾in) in diameter and about 3cm (1¼in) deep. Retain the cut-out piece of sponge. Spoon about 1 teaspoon of the blackcurrant jam into the hollow. Replace the cut-out piece of sponge, trimming to fit and pressing down gently to ensure that the top is level with the rest of the cake.

11. Spoon generous amounts of the frosting onto each cupcake, then gently smooth over with a palette knife, making a swirl at the top if you wish. Top each cupcake with a liquorice sweet.

Good-quality shop-bought panettone dotted with candied fruit pieces works best for these cupcakes. This is what we use and they come out a treat.

Panettone Cupcakes

MAKES 12–16 CUPCAKES

FOR THE CUSTARD

330ml (11½ fl oz) WHOLE MILK

3 LARGE EGG YOLKS

60g (2oz) CASTER SUGAR

20g (¾oz) PLAIN FLOUR

20g (¾oz) CORNFLOUR

150ml (5½ fl oz) DOUBLE CREAM

FOR THE SPONGE

70g (2½oz) UNSALTED BUTTER, SOFTENED

210g (7½oz) PLAIN FLOUR

250g (9oz) CASTER SUGAR

1 tbsp BAKING POWDER

½ tsp SALT

210ml (7½ fl oz) WHOLE MILK

2 LARGE EGGS

1 tsp VANILLA EXTRACT

150g (5½oz) PANETTONE, CUT INTO CUBES

FOR THE DECORATION

50g (1¾oz) PANETTONE, CUT INTO CUBES

ICING SUGAR, FOR DUSTING

EQUIPMENT

ONE OR TWO 12-HOLE DEEP MUFFIN TINS

1. Preheat the oven to 170°C (325°F), Gas mark 3, and line the muffin tins with paper muffin cases to make the number you require.

2. To make the custard, place the milk in a saucepan and bring to the boil. In a bowl, mix together the egg yolks, sugar, flour and cornflour to make a paste, adding 1 tablespoon of the hot milk to thin if necessary.

3. When the milk has boiled, remove the pan from the heat and mix 4–5 tablespoons with the egg and flour paste, then pour this back into the pan with the remaining hot milk and return to the heat.

4. Bring back up to the boil, whisking constantly, and continue to boil for a further 3–4 minutes to ensure the flour and cornflour are fully cooked. However, be careful not to overcook or the eggs may begin to scramble. Remove from the heat and immediately pour the custard into a baking tray. Cover directly with cling film and set aside to cool completely.

5. In a freestanding electric mixer with the paddle attachment or using a hand-held electric whisk, mix the butter, flour, sugar, baking powder and salt together until they form a crumb-like consistency.

6. In a separate jug, mix together the milk, eggs and vanilla extract by hand.

7. With the mixer or whisk on a slow speed, gradually pour half of the liquid into the crumb mixture and mix thoroughly until combined. Then turn up the speed to medium and beat until the batter is smooth and thick with no lumps. Scrape down the sides of the bowl as you go. Once all lumps have gone, reduce the speed and gradually pour in the remaining liquid from the jug, continuing to mix until the batter is smooth and combined.

Recipe continues …

8. Place 3–4 cubes of panettone into each paper case. Spoon the batter into the cases, filling them two-thirds full. Using a 50ml (1¾fl oz) ice-cream scoop can make this process easier and will result in even cupcakes. The batter should roughly cover the panettone.

9. Bake for approximately 20–25 minutes or until golden brown and the sponge bounces back when lightly touched. Leave to cool slightly before removing from the tin and placing on a wire rack to cool completely before frosting.

10. Meanwhile, place the remaining cubes of panettone onto a baking tray. Toast them in the oven at 170°C (325°F), Gas mark 3, for about 3–5 minutes. These brown very quickly so don't walk away from the oven. Move them around the tray with a wooden spoon to make sure they are evenly toasted.

11. To finish the custard, pour the double cream into a medium bowl. Using the freestanding electric mixer with the whisk attachment or the hand-held electric whisk, beat the cream until it forms soft peaks. Place the cooled custard into a medium bowl. With the mixer or whisk on a slow speed, mix the custard until it is smooth. Using a spatula, gradually fold the whipped cream into the custard.

12. Spoon generous amounts of the custard onto each cupcake, then gently smooth over with a palette knife, making a swirl at the top if you wish. Top each cupcake with 2–3 pieces of toasted panettone and lightly dust with icing sugar.

Salty-sweet — a combination that can't be beat! Using a pinch of good-quality sea salt gives the frosting the crunchy saltiness that makes these cupcakes just perfect.

Salted Caramel Cupcakes

MAKES 12–16 CUPCAKES

FOR THE SPONGE

70g (2½oz) UNSALTED BUTTER, SOFTENED

170g (6oz) PLAIN FLOUR

250g (9oz) CASTER SUGAR

50g (1¾oz) COCOA POWDER, SIFTED

1 tbsp BAKING POWDER

½ tsp SALT

210ml (7½fl oz) WHOLE MILK

2 LARGE EGGS

FOR THE FROSTING

670g (1lb 7oz) ICING SUGAR, SIFTED

210g (7½oz) UNSALTED BUTTER, SOFTENED

70ml (2½fl oz) WHOLE MILK

30g (1oz) TINNED CARAMEL OR *DULCE DE LECHE*

PINCH OF GOOD-QUALITY SEA SALT (SUCH AS MALDON)

Ingredients continue ...

1. Preheat the oven to 170°C (325°F), Gas mark 3, and line the muffin tins with paper muffin cases to make the number you require.

2. First make the sponge. In a freestanding electric mixer with the paddle attachment or using a hand-held electric whisk, mix the butter, flour, sugar, cocoa powder, baking powder and salt together until they form a crumb-like consistency.

3. In a jug, mix together the milk and eggs by hand.

4. With the mixer or whisk on a slow speed, gradually pour half of the liquid into the crumb mixture and mix thoroughly until combined. Raise the speed to medium and beat until the batter is smooth and thick, with no lumps. Scrape down the sides of the bowl now and then. Once all lumps are gone, turn the speed back down and gradually pour in the remaining liquid, continuing to mix until the batter is smooth and combined.

5. Spoon the batter into the prepared paper cases, filling them two-thirds full. Using a 50ml (1¾fl oz) ice-cream scoop can make this process easier and will result in even cupcakes.

6. Bake for 20–25 minutes or until the sponge bounces back when lightly touched. Leave to cool slightly before removing from the tin and placing on a wire rack to cool completely before frosting.

7. Using the freestanding electric mixer with the paddle attachment or the hand-held electric whisk, gradually mix the icing sugar and butter together on a low speed until combined and there are no large lumps of butter. Gradually add the milk while mixing on a slow speed. Add the *dulce de leche* and sea salt and mix thoroughly. Turn up the speed and beat until light and fluffy.

Recipe continues ...

FOR THE FILLING AND DECORATION

100g (3½oz) TINNED CARAMEL OR *DULCE DE LECHE*

PINCH OF GOOD-QUALITY SEA SALT

EQUIPMENT

ONE OR TWO 12-HOLE DEEP MUFFIN TINS

8. Once the cupcakes are cool, use a sharp knife to make a hollow in the centre of each cupcake, approximately 2cm (¾in) in diameter and about 3cm (1¼in) deep. Retain the cut-out piece of sponge. Spoon about 1 teaspoon of the *dulce de leche* into the hollow. Replace the cut-out piece of sponge, trimming to fit and pressing down gently to ensure that the top is level with the rest of the cake.

9. Spoon generous amounts of the frosting onto each cupcake, then gently smooth over with a palette knife, making a swirl at the top if you wish. To finish, spoon about 1 teaspoon of *dulce de leche* on the top of each frosted cupcake, swirling it slightly into the frosting, and add a light sprinkling of sea salt.

The tartness of cranberries works wonderfully with the sweetness of white chocolate. These pretty cupcakes make a lovely festive alternative to traditional Christmas cake.

White Chocolate & Cranberry Cupcakes

MAKES 12–16 CUPCAKES

FOR THE SPONGE

70g (2½oz) UNSALTED BUTTER, SOFTENED

210g (7½oz) PLAIN FLOUR

250g (9oz) CASTER SUGAR

1 tbsp BAKING POWDER

½ tsp SALT

210ml (7½fl oz) WHOLE MILK

2 LARGE EGGS

60g (2oz) DRIED CRANBERRIES

1 tsp GRATED ORANGE ZEST

FOR THE FROSTING

60g (2oz) WHITE CHOCOLATE, CHOPPED

500g (1lb 2oz) ICING SUGAR, SIFTED

160g (5½oz) UNSALTED BUTTER, SOFTENED

50ml (1¾fl oz) WHOLE MILK

FOR THE DECORATION

20g (¾oz) DRIED CRANBERRIES

1 tsp GRATED ORANGE ZEST

EQUIPMENT

ONE OR TWO 12-HOLE DEEP MUFFIN TINS

1. Preheat the oven to 170°C (325°F), Gas mark 3, and line the muffin tins with paper muffin cases to make the number you require.

2. First make the sponge. In a freestanding electric mixer with the paddle attachment or using a hand-held electric whisk, mix the butter, flour, sugar, baking powder and salt together until they form a crumb-like consistency.

3. In a jug, mix together the milk and eggs by hand.

4. With the mixer or whisk on a slow speed, gradually pour half of the liquid into the crumb mixture and mix thoroughly until combined. Turn up the speed to medium and beat until the batter is smooth and thick, with no lumps. Scrape down the sides of the bowl occasionally. Once any lumps have gone, turn the speed back down and gradually pour in the remaining liquid, continuing to mix until the batter is smooth and combined.

5. Add the cranberries and orange zest, and mix through the batter, making sure they are evenly distributed. Spoon the batter into the prepared paper cases, filling them two-thirds full. Using a 50ml (1¾fl oz) ice-cream scoop can make this process easier and will result in even cupcakes.

6. Bake for 20–25 minutes or until the sponge bounces back when lightly touched. Leave to cool slightly before removing from the tin and placing on a wire rack to cool completely before frosting.

7. To make the frosting, melt the white chocolate in a microwave-safe bowl in the microwave or in a heatproof bowl set over a pan of simmering water.

8. Using the freestanding electric mixer with the paddle attachment or the hand-held electric whisk, gradually mix the icing sugar and butter together on a low speed until combined and there are no large lumps of butter. Gradually pour in the milk while mixing on a slow speed. When all the liquid is incorporated, turn the mixer up to a high speed and beat the frosting until light and fluffy. Add the melted white chocolate to the frosting, mix well until the frosting is even and smooth.

9. Spoon generous amounts of the frosting onto each cupcake, then gently smooth over with a palette knife, making a swirl at the top if you wish. Top each cupcake with a couple of dried cranberries and a sprinkling of orange zest.

Using shop-bought cookies for these cakes works really well and helps save time, but if you want to go all out, then bake your favourite double chocolate cookies and use them instead.

Cookies & Cream Cupcakes

MAKES 12–16 CUPCAKES

FOR THE SPONGE

70g (2½oz) UNSALTED BUTTER, SOFTENED

170g (6oz) PLAIN FLOUR

250g (9oz) CASTER SUGAR

50g (1¾oz) COCOA POWDER, SIFTED

1 tbsp BAKING POWDER

½ tsp SALT

210ml (7½fl oz) WHOLE MILK

2 LARGE EGGS

12–16 DOUBLE CHOCOLATE COOKIES
(SUCH AS OREOS OR DOUBLE CHOCOLATE MARYLANDS)

FOR THE FROSTING

500g (1lb 2oz) ICING SUGAR, SIFTED

160g (5½oz) UNSALTED BUTTER, SOFTENED

60ml (2fl oz) WHOLE MILK

8 DOUBLE CHOCOLATE COOKIES,
CRUSHED INTO ROUGH PIECES AND CRUMBS

FOR THE DECORATION

4–5 DOUBLE CHOCOLATE COOKIES,
CRUSHED INTO CRUMBS

EQUIPMENT

ONE OR TWO 12-HOLE DEEP MUFFIN TINS

1. Preheat the oven to 170°C (325°F), Gas mark 3, and line the muffin tins with paper muffin cases to make the number you require.

2. First make the sponge. In a freestanding electric mixer with the paddle attachment or using a hand-held electric whisk, mix the butter, flour, sugar, cocoa powder, baking powder and salt together until they form a crumb-like consistency.

3. In a jug, mix together the milk and eggs by hand.

4. With the mixer or whisk on a slow speed, gradually pour half of the liquid into the crumb mixture and mix thoroughly until combined. Raise the speed to medium and mix until the batter is smooth and thick, with no lumps. Scrape down the sides of the bowl as you go. Once all lumps are gone, turn the speed back down and gradually pour in the remaining liquid, continuing to mix until the batter is smooth and combined.

5. Spoon the batter into the prepared paper cases, filling them two-thirds full. Using a 50ml (1¾fl oz) ice-cream scoop can make this process easier and will result in even cupcakes.

6. Break each cookie into quarters and place four pieces of cookie in each unbaked cupcake. Bake for about 20–25 minutes or until the sponge bounces back when lightly touched. Leave to cool slightly before removing from the tin and placing on a wire rack to cool completely before frosting.

7. Using the freestanding electric mixer with the paddle attachment or the hand-held electric whisk, gradually mix the icing sugar and butter together on a low speed until combined and there are no large lumps of butter. Gradually pour the milk into the butter and icing sugar while mixing on a slow speed. When all the liquid is incorporated, turn the mixer up to a high speed and beat the frosting until light and fluffy. Add the double chocolate cookie crumbs and mix well until evenly distributed through the frosting.

8. Once the cupcakes are cool, spoon generous amounts of the frosting onto each cupcake, then gently smooth over with a palette knife, making a swirl at the top if you wish. This can be difficult with the cookie pieces in the frosting, so expect a messier look. Top each cupcake with a coating of cookie crumbs.

We couldn't stop snacking on these sweet peanut sweets while testing these moreish cupcakes, but we recommend you try and save some for decoration! Using crunchy peanut butter gives added texture to the frosting.

Sweet Peanut Cupcakes

MAKES 12–16 CUPCAKES

FOR THE SPONGE

70g (2½oz) UNSALTED BUTTER, SOFTENED

210g (7½oz) PLAIN FLOUR

250g (9oz) CASTER SUGAR

1 tbsp BAKING POWDER

½ tsp SALT

210ml (7½fl oz) WHOLE MILK

2 LARGE EGGS

40g (1½oz) CRUNCHY PEANUT BUTTER

FOR THE FROSTING

500g (1lb 2oz) ICING SUGAR, SIFTED

160g (5½oz) UNSALTED BUTTER, SOFTENED

50ml (1¾fl oz) WHOLE MILK

30g (1oz) CRUNCHY PEANUT BUTTER

FOR THE DECORATION

8 SWEET PEANUT SWEETS, ROUGHLY CHOPPED INTO SMALL BITS

EQUIPMENT

ONE OR TWO 12-HOLE DEEP MUFFIN TINS

1. Preheat the oven to 170°C (325°F), Gas mark 3, and line the muffin tins with paper muffin cases to make the number you require.

2. First make the sponge. In a freestanding electric mixer with the paddle attachment or using a hand-held electric whisk, mix the butter, flour, sugar, baking powder and salt together until they form a crumb-like consistency.

3. In a jug, mix together the milk and eggs by hand.

4. With the mixer or whisk on a slow speed, gradually pour half of the liquid into the crumb mixture and mix thoroughly until combined. Raise the speed to medium and beat until the batter is smooth and thick, with no lumps. Scrape down the sides of the bowl from time to time. Once all lumps are gone, turn the speed back down and gradually pour in the remaining liquid, continuing to mix until the batter is smooth and combined.

5. Add the peanut butter and mix through, making sure it is evenly mixed through the batter.

6. Spoon the batter into the prepared paper cases, filling them two-thirds full. Using a 50ml (1¾fl oz) ice-cream scoop can make this process easier and will result in even cupcakes. Bake for 20–25 minutes or until the sponge bounces back when lightly touched. Leave to cool slightly before removing from the tin and placing on a wire rack to cool completely before frosting.

7. Using the freestanding electric mixer with the paddle attachment or the hand-held electric whisk, gradually mix the icing sugar and butter together on a low speed until combined and there are no large lumps of butter. Gradually pour in the milk while mixing on a slow speed. When all the liquid is incorporated, turn the mixer up to a high speed and beat the frosting until light and fluffy. Add the peanut butter and mix well until the frosting is even and smooth.

8. Spoon generous amounts of the frosting onto each cupcake, then gently smooth over with a palette knife, making a swirl at the top if you wish. Top each cupcake with a sprinkling of the chopped peanut sweets.

Using real strawberries just does not work in this recipe; it needs the strawberry powder to unequivocally shout 'milkshake'! Edible straws are available from specialist shops and will wow your friends and family, although these cakes are still utterly delicious without them.

Strawberry Milkshake Cupcakes

MAKES 12–16 CUPCAKES

FOR THE SPONGE

70g (2½oz) UNSALTED BUTTER, SOFTENED

210g (7½oz) PLAIN FLOUR

250g (9oz) CASTER SUGAR

1 tbsp BAKING POWDER

½ tsp SALT

210ml (7½fl oz) WHOLE MILK

2 LARGE EGGS

40g (1½oz) STRAWBERRY MILKSHAKE POWDER

FOR THE FROSTING

500g (1lb 2oz) ICING SUGAR, SIFTED

160g (5½oz) UNSALTED BUTTER, SOFTENED

50ml (1¾fl oz) WHOLE MILK

100g (3½oz) STRAWBERRY MILKSHAKE POWDER

FOR THE DECORATION

STRAWBERRY MILKSHAKE POWDER, TO SPRINKLE

EQUIPMENT

ONE OR TWO 12-HOLE DEEP MUFFIN TINS

1. Preheat the oven to 170°C (325°F), Gas mark 3, and line the muffin tins with paper muffin cases to make the number you require.

2. First make the sponge. In a freestanding electric mixer with the paddle attachment or using a hand-held electric whisk, mix the butter, flour, sugar, baking powder and salt together until they form a crumb-like consistency.

3. In a jug, mix together the milk, eggs and strawberry milkshake powder by hand.

4. With the mixer or whisk on a slow speed, gradually pour half of the liquid into the crumb mixture and mix thoroughly until combined. Raise the speed to medium and beat until the batter is smooth and thick, with no lumps. Scrape down the sides of the bowl now and then. Once all lumps are gone, turn the speed back down and gradually pour in the remaining liquid, continuing to mix until the batter is smooth and combined.

5. Spoon the batter into the prepared paper cases, filling them two-thirds full. Using a 50ml (1¾fl oz) ice-cream scoop can make this process easier and will result in even cupcakes.

6. Bake for 20–25 minutes or until the sponge bounces back when lightly touched. Leave to cool slightly before removing from the tin and placing on a wire rack to cool completely before frosting.

7. Using the freestanding electric mixer with the paddle attachment or the hand-held electric whisk, gradually mix the icing sugar and butter together on a low speed until combined and there are no large lumps of butter. In a jug, mix the milk and strawberry milkshake powder together. Gradually pour the liquid into the frosting, while mixing on a slow speed. When all the liquid is incorporated, turn the mixer up to a high speed and beat the frosting until light and fluffy.

8. Spoon generous amounts of the frosting onto each cupcake, then gently smooth over with a palette knife, making a swirl at the top if you wish. Top each cupcake with a sprinkling of strawberry milkshake powder.

CAKES, CHEESECAKES & ROULADES

CAKES,
CHEESECAKES
& ROULADES

We like almond cake, but by putting a giant home-made macaroon on top, we absolutely love it! Do make sure that the macaroon doesn't go into the oven earlier than instructed otherwise it will burn.

Almond Cake with Macaroon Top

SERVES 8–10

FOR THE SPONGE

80g (3oz) FINE YELLOW CORNMEAL

80g (3oz) PLAIN FLOUR

1 tsp BAKING POWDER

115g (4oz) UNSALTED BUTTER, SOFTENED

50g (1¾oz) MARZIPAN, CUBED

200g (7oz) ICING SUGAR

4 LARGE EGG YOLKS

2 LARGE EGGS

½ tsp VANILLA EXTRACT

60g (2oz) SOURED CREAM

FOR THE TOPPING

2 LARGE EGG WHITES

125g (4½oz) CASTER SUGAR

125g (4½oz) GROUND ALMONDS

EQUIPMENT

ONE 20cm (8in) DIAMETER SPRING-FORM CAKE TIN

1. Preheat the oven to 170°C (325°F), Gas mark 3, and line the cake tin with baking parchment.

2. Sift together the cornmeal, flour and baking powder.

3. In a freestanding electric mixer with the paddle attachment or using a hand-held electric whisk, beat the butter and marzipan until smooth. Add the icing sugar and mix until light and fluffy. Add the egg yolks and eggs one at a time, mixing well after each addition. Scrape down the sides of the bowl.

4. With the mixer or whisk on a slow speed, add the vanilla extract, soured cream and dry ingredients, mixing until combined. Pour the batter into the prepared cake tin and bake for 30 minutes.

5. While the cake is in the oven, make the macaroon topping. In the freestanding electric mixer with the whisk attachment or using the hand-held electric whisk, whip up the egg whites until they form soft peaks. With the mixer or whisk on a medium speed, add the caster sugar to the egg whites a little at a time. Once all the sugar has been added, the meringue should be white and glossy. Carefully fold the ground almonds into the meringue. It is normal for the meringue to lose some of its volume at this point.

6. When the cake has baked for 30 minutes and is almost baked through, carefully remove from the oven and spread the macaroon topping over the top. Continue to bake for a further 15 minutes or until the macaroon topping is an even golden colour and has formed a crust on top.

7. Allow the cake to cool for 30 minutes, then remove from the cake tin and leave to cool completely before serving.

* This cake can be made without the macaroon top.

* A spring-form tin is essential otherwise the cake won't turn out.

Our fruity variation of the more traditional Boston Cream Pie.
We've made it even more indulgent in true Hummingbird Bakery style.

Banana Boston Cream Cake

SERVES 8–10

FOR THE SPONGE

100g (3½oz) UNSALTED BUTTER, SOFTENED

150g (5½oz) CASTER SUGAR

2 LARGE EGGS

1 MEDIUM BANANA, MASHED

125g (4½oz) SOURED CREAM

1 tsp VANILLA EXTRACT

300g (10½oz) PLAIN FLOUR

½ tsp SALT

¾ tsp BAKING POWDER

1 tsp BICARBONATE OF SODA

FOR THE CUSTARD

250ml (9fl oz) WHOLE MILK

1 tsp VANILLA EXTRACT

3 EGG YOLKS

50g (1¾oz) CASTER SUGAR

15g (½oz) PLAIN FLOUR

15g (½oz) CORNFLOUR

FOR THE CHOCOLATE GANACHE

400ml (14fl oz) DOUBLE CREAM

400g (14oz) DARK CHOCOLATE, CHOPPED

FOR THE DECORATION

CHOCOLATE SHAVINGS (MINIMUM 70% COCOA SOLIDS)

Ingredients continue ...

1. Preheat the oven to 170°C (325°F), Gas mark 3, and line the cake tins with baking parchment.

2. Using a freestanding electric mixer with the paddle attachment or a hand-held electric whisk, cream the butter and sugar together until light and fluffy. Add the eggs one at a time, mixing well and scraping down the sides of the bowl after each addition.

3. In a jug, mix together the mashed banana, soured cream and vanilla extract. Sift together the flour, salt, baking powder and bicarbonate of soda.

4. With the mixer or whisk on a slow speed, pour the soured cream mixture into the creamed butter mixture. Mix well to ensure all the ingredients are incorporated. Add the dry ingredients and mix until the batter is even and smooth.

5. Divide the batter evenly between the two prepared cake tins. Bake for 25–35 minutes or until the sponge bounces back if touched lightly. Remove from the tins and allow to cool completely before finishing.

6. Meanwhile, make the custard filling. Bring the milk and vanilla extract to the boil in a medium pan. In a medium bowl, mix together the egg yolks, sugar, flour and cornflour to form a paste. A small amount of the warming milk can be added to loosen the paste.

7. Once the milk is ready, pour a small amount of milk onto the paste and mix. Add the paste to the remaining milk and put it back on the heat, whisking all the time until it forms a thick custard. This must gently boil for at least 4–5 minutes until the flour is fully cooked. However, be careful not to overcook or the eggs may begin to scramble. Pour the cooked custard onto a baking tray and cover immediately with cling film. This will prevent a skin forming. Set aside to cool completely.

Recipe continues ...

8. Once the sponge layers feel cool to the touch you can assemble the cake. In the freestanding electric mixer with the paddle attachment or using the hand-held electric whisk on a slow speed, mix the custard until it is smooth. Place the first sponge layer on a plate or cake card and top with the cold custard. Smooth the custard out using a palette knife, adding a little more if needed. Sandwich the second layer on top. Wrap the sides of the cake tightly in cling film. Place the cake in the fridge to set for approximately 45 minutes.

9. While the cake is in the fridge, make the ganache topping. In a medium pan, heat the double cream until almost boiling. Place the chopped dark chocolate into a medium mixing bowl. Pour the hot cream over the chocolate. Stir until all the chocolate has melted and the ganache is smooth and shiny.

10. Put a wire cooling rack over a baking tray (a deep one, ideally) to catch the ganache topping. Place the chilled cake on the cooling rack and remove the cling film. Pour the ganache topping over the top of the cake. It will run down the sides of the cake and any extra will collect in the baking tray. This process can be repeated until the cake is evenly coated. Put the cake back in the fridge for about 40 minutes for the ganache to set. The cake can then be decorated with chocolate shavings if desired.

∗ If your banana isn't very ripe, add another to the mixture to obtain a stronger banana flavour.

Everyone loves a lemon loaf cake and we've made this version extra special by using yeast to make a sweet dough and adding a wonderfully tangy icing. It takes more time and effort, but the result is pure lemon heaven in a loaf tin. This is best eaten warm and on the day of baking — it will go stale quite quickly if stored.

Sweet Dough Lemon Loaf

SERVES 8–10

FOR THE DOUGH
75ml (2½fl oz) LUKEWARM WHOLE MILK
60ml (2fl oz) TEPID WATER
½ tsp SALT
50g (1¾oz) CASTER SUGAR
2¼ tsp DRIED ACTIVE YEAST
350g (12oz) PLAIN FLOUR, PLUS EXTRA FOR DUSTING
55g (2oz) UNSALTED BUTTER, PLUS EXTRA FOR GREASING
2 LARGE EGGS, BEATEN
2 tsp VANILLA EXTRACT

FOR THE FILLING
60g (2oz) UNSALTED BUTTER
100g (3½oz) CASTER SUGAR
GRATED ZEST OF 3 LEMONS

FOR THE TOPPING
90g (3oz) FULL-FAT CREAM CHEESE (SUCH AS PHILADELPHIA)
40g (1½oz) ICING SUGAR, SIFTED
1 tbsp LEMON JUICE
GRATED ZEST OF 1 LEMON, PLUS EXTRA TO DECORATE
1 tbsp WHOLE MILK

EQUIPMENT
ONE 900g (2lb) LOAF TIN

1. Grease the loaf tin with butter and dust with flour.

2. In a small jug, mix together the warm milk, water, salt, 1 teaspoon of the sugar and the dried active yeast. Set this aside to ferment for about 30 minutes or until it forms a foam on the surface.

3. In a large mixing bowl, mix together the flour and remaining sugar and make a well in the centre. Melt the butter in a microwave-safe bowl in the microwave or in a small pan on the stove. When the yeast liquid is ready, add the eggs, vanilla extract and melted butter to the yeast mixture.

4. Pour the liquids into the centre of the dry ingredients and mix together using a spatula or wooden spoon to form a dough. Turn the dough out onto a lightly floured surface and knead for approximately 5 minutes or until the dough is smooth and even.

5. Place the dough in a lightly floured bowl, cover tightly with cling film and allow to prove in a warm place. This should take about 45 minutes or until the dough has doubled in size.

6. While the dough is proving, make the lemon sugar filling. Melt the butter in a microwave-safe bowl in the microwave or in a small pan on the stove. In a medium bowl, mix the sugar, lemon zest and melted butter together. Set this aside for later use. Try and keep it somewhere warm so that the butter doesn't set.

7. Once the dough has proved, remove it from the bowl. Gently knock the dough back. Roll it out on a lightly floured surface until it is about 30 x 38cm (12 x 15in). Using a sharp knife, cut the dough lengthways into four equal strips.

Recipe continues …

8. Using a pastry brush, coat each strip with the lemon sugar filling. Carefully lift the strips and pile them neatly one on top of another, and then cut the pile of strips into six equal square stacks. Carefully lift each stack and place it into the tin, cut side facing up. Place each stack next to one another to fill the length of the tin, packing them together like a sliced loaf.

9. Wrap the tin in cling film and set aside for the dough to rise again. This should take approximately 30–40 minutes or until the dough has doubled in size.

10. Preheat the oven to 170°C (325°F), Gas mark 3, and bake the loaf for approximately 30–35 minutes or until an even golden brown. Set aside to cool slightly.

11. To make the lemon cream cheese topping, use a freestanding electric mixer with the paddle attachment or a hand-held electric whisk to mix the cream cheese and icing sugar together just until smooth. Add the lemon juice, zest and milk. Mix well until creamy and smooth.

12. Once the loaf has cooled slightly, remove it from the tin and top with the lemon topping, scattering over extra lemon zest to finish. Serve warm or at room temperature.

This is a fridge-set cheesecake made using gelatine. Vegetarian-friendly gelatine can be used, but do check the package for instructions and conversions. We use shop-bought biscuits for an easy-to-make and tasty crunchy base.

Peanut Butter Cheesecake

SERVES 10-12

FOR THE BISCUIT BASE

200g (7oz) NUTTY CHOCOLATE CHIP BISCUITS

75g (2½oz) UNSALTED BUTTER, MELTED

FOR THE CHEESECAKE TOPPING

400g (14oz) FULL-FAT CREAM CHEESE (SUCH AS PHILADELPHIA)

150g (5½oz) CASTER SUGAR

4 LARGE EGG YOLKS

6 LEAVES OF GELATINE

150g (5½oz) CRUNCHY PEANUT BUTTER

250ml (9fl oz) DOUBLE CREAM

FOR THE PEANUT BRITTLE

100g (3½oz) UNSALTED ROASTED PEANUTS

200g (7oz) CASTER SUGAR

50ML (1¾fl oz) WATER

EQUIPMENT

ONE 23cm (9in) DIAMETER SPRING-FORM CAKE TIN

1. First line the cake tin with baking parchment.

2. In a food processor with the blade attachment, blitz the biscuits into rough crumbs. Pour the melted butter into the crumbs and blitz again until all the crumbs are coated in butter. Press the biscuit crumb mixture into the base of the prepared tin. Leave in the fridge for the base to set for approximately 30–40 minutes.

3. In a freestanding electric mixer with the paddle attachment or using a hand-held electric whisk, beat the cream cheese, caster sugar and egg yolks together until smooth.

4. In a medium bowl, soak the gelatine leaves in cold water. Allow them to soften completely.

5. Melt the peanut butter in a microwave-safe bowl in the microwave or in a small pan over a gentle heat, stirring continuously so that it doesn't catch on the bottom.

6. Remove the gelatine leaves from the water, squeezing them slightly to get rid of any excess water. Dissolve the gelatine in the melted peanut butter. Add approximately 3 tablespoons of the cream cheese mixture to the peanut butter and mix thoroughly. Repeat this process a couple of times to adjust the warm peanut butter to the cold cream cheese mixture without the gelatine setting. Then add the peanut butter mixture to the remaining cream cheese mixture, stirring until it is smooth and even.

7. In a separate bowl, whip up the double cream until it forms soft peaks. Gently fold the whipped cream into the peanut cream cheese mixture.

8. Pour the cheesecake filling onto the prepared biscuit base, then leave to set in the fridge, preferably overnight but for a minimum of 4 hours, until completely set.

Recipe continues ...

9. While the cheesecake is setting, make the peanut brittle. Line a baking tray with baking parchment and evenly spread the roasted peanuts over the tray.

10. Put the sugar and water in a medium saucepan and heat gently, stirring until the sugar has dissolved. Then bring the syrup to the boil, allowing it to boil for 15–20 minutes until it has developed into a rich golden caramel. Do not stir while the mixture is boiling or the caramel will crystallise; just gently swirl the pan from time to time.

11. Wearing oven gloves, carefully pour the hot caramel over the nuts, trying to coat them all evenly. Leave this to cool and set completely.

12. Once the brittle has set, break it into rough pieces. Using a food processor with a blade attachment, blitz the brittle into rough crumbs. Try not to leave too many big pieces as these will be difficult to eat.

13. Once the cheesecake has set, carefully remove it from the spring-form tin, and transfer it onto a plate or tray. Sprinkle the brittle over the top of the cheesecake just before serving.

This show-stopping cake looks so amazing when finished that it is ideal for special events or wowing friends on their birthdays. Once they've tasted this cake they will want you to make it every year.

Chocolate Cake with Vanilla Meringue Frosting

SERVES 10-12

FOR THE DECORATION

60g (2oz) MILK CHOCOLATE

50g (1¾oz) WHITE CHOCOLATE

FOR THE SPONGE

170g (6oz) UNSALTED BUTTER, SOFTENED

350g (12oz) SOFT LIGHT BROWN SUGAR

3 LARGE EGGS

80g (3oz) DARK CHOCOLATE (MINIMUM 70% COCOA SOLIDS)

225g (8oz) PLAIN FLOUR

1½ tsp BICARBONATE OF SODA

½ tsp SALT

225g (8oz) SOURED CREAM

2 tsp VANILLA EXTRACT

2 tbsp INSTANT COFFEE MIXED WITH 240ml (8½fl oz) BOILING WATER OR 240ml (8½fl oz) ESPRESSO COFFEE (IF YOU HAVE A MACHINE)

Ingredients continue ...

1. To make the chocolate decoration, melt the milk chocolate and white chocolate separately in two small bowls, either in microwave-safe dishes in the microwave or set over small pans of simmering water.

2. Turn one of the cake tins upside down and place a thin piece of plastic over the top of the tin (A4 laminating pouches work very well, pulled apart to make two sheets). Place a blob of the melted milk chocolate in the centre and a blob of the white chocolate next to the milk chocolate.

3. Using the back of a spoon, gently spread the chocolate around, marbling the two colours in a round disc that is the same size as the base of the cake tin. Once done, carefully lift the plastic sheet and set aside on a flat surface for the chocolate to set completely.

4. Preheat the oven to 170°C (325°F), Gas mark 3, and line the cake tins with baking parchment.

5. In a freestanding electric mixer with the paddle attachment or using a hand-held electric whisk, cream the butter and the sugar together until light and fluffy. Add the eggs one at a time, scraping down the sides of the bowl and mixing well after each addition.

6. Melt the dark chocolate in a microwave-safe bowl in the microwave or in a glass bowl set over a small pan of simmering water. With the mixer or whisk on a slow speed, pour the melted chocolate into the creamed butter and sugar mixture.

7. In a medium bowl, sift together the flour, bicarbonate of soda and salt. In a jug, mix together the soured cream, vanilla extract and coffee.

8. With the mixer or whisk on a slow speed, add the dry ingredients to the creamed butter and sugar in alternating additions with the coffee mixture. Once everything has been added, scrape down the sides of the bowl and mix well to form a smooth, even batter.

Recipe continues ...

FOR THE FROSTING

300g (10½oz) CASTER SUGAR

80g (3oz) GOLDEN SYRUP

120ml (4fl oz) WATER

4 LARGE EGG WHITES

½ tsp CREAM OF TARTAR

1 tsp VANILLA EXTRACT

EQUIPMENT

THREE 20cm (8in) DIAMETER LOOSE-BOTTOMED
SANDWICH TINS

SUGAR THERMOMETER

SHEET OF PLASTIC, SUCH AS A LAMINATING POUCH

9. Divide the batter evenly amongst the three prepared tins. Bake for approximately 20–25 minutes or until the sponge bounces back when lightly touched. Remove from the tins and allow to cool completely before frosting.

10. Next, make the meringue frosting. In a medium saucepan, dissolve the sugar and golden syrup in the water. Bring this to the boil. This must boil, without stirring, until the sugar reaches the soft ball stage (a little bit of the syrup dropped into cold water will form a soft ball). If you have one, use a sugar thermometer to check when it is ready — it needs to reach 115°C (239°F).

11. Meanwhile, in the freestanding electric mixer using a whisk attachment or in a large bowl with a hand-held electric whisk, whip up the egg whites with the cream of tartar and vanilla extract. This should be whipped up only until it is just beginning to become white and frothy.

12. When the syrup is ready, carefully pour it onto the egg whites while the mixer or whisk is on a medium speed, gradually increasing the speed while pouring. Once all the syrup has been added, turn the mixer speed to high and let the meringue whip up. It will become very white and glossy and the bowl will be warm to the touch. Let it continue to mix until the base of the bowl has cooled to lukewarm.

13. Once the sponge layers feel cool to the touch, you can assemble and frost the cake. Place the first layer on a plate or cake card and top with 3–4 tablespoons of meringue frosting. Smooth the frosting out using a palette knife, adding a little more if needed. Sandwich the second layer on top, then add more frosting, followed by the third layer of cake.

14. Next frost the sides and top of the cake, covering it completely so that no sponge is showing.

15. Carefully peel the plastic off the chocolate disc and place the disc on the top of the cake to finish. If the chocolate disc breaks, this is absolutely not a problem — just break it into more pieces and decorate the top of the cake with these.

This simple-to-make but pretty cheesecake is just full of flavour.
Using dried sour cherries is best as it gives an added tang to the taste.

Chocolate & Cherry Cheesecake Swirl Cake

SERVES 10-12

FOR THE CHOCOLATE SPONGE

70g (2½oz) COCOA POWDER, SIFTED

180ml (6½fl oz) HOT WATER

260g (9oz) PLAIN FLOUR, PLUS EXTRA FOR DUSTING

1½ tsp BICARBONATE OF SODA

½ tsp BAKING POWDER

½ tsp SALT

180g (6½oz) SOURED CREAM

170g (6oz) UNSALTED BUTTER, SOFTENED

380g (13oz) CASTER SUGAR

3 LARGE EGGS

FOR THE CHERRY CHEESECAKE SWIRL

450g (1lb) FULL-FAT CREAM CHEESE (SUCH AS PHILADELPHIA)

100g (3½oz) CASTER SUGAR

2 LARGE EGGS

1½ tsp VANILLA EXTRACT

40g (1½oz) DRIED SOUR CHERRIES, ROUGHLY CHOPPED

80g (3oz) BLACK CHERRY JAM, TO GLAZE

EQUIPMENT

ONE 25cm (10in) DIAMETER NON-STICK RING CAKE TIN

PIPING BAG WITH A WIDE NOZZLE

1. Preheat the oven to 170°C (325°F), Gas mark 3, grease the cake tin with butter and dust with flour.

2. In a small bowl, mix together the cocoa powder and hot water, stirring until well combined and a thick chocolate liquid is formed.

3. Sift together the flour, bicarbonate of soda, baking powder and salt. In a jug, mix the soured cream and chocolate liquid together.

4. In a freestanding electric mixer with the paddle attachment or using a hand-held electric whisk, cream the butter and sugar together until light and fluffy. Add the eggs one at a time, mixing well and scraping down the bowl after each addition.

5. With the mixer or whisk on a medium speed, pour in the soured cream mixture. Add the dry ingredients and mix well to form a smooth, even dough. Set aside to use later.

6. Next, make the cherry cheesecake. In the freestanding electric mixer with the paddle attachment or using the hand-held electric whisk, mix the cream cheese and sugar until smooth. Add the eggs one at a time, mixing well after each addition. Stir in the vanilla extract and chopped cherries by hand, making sure the cherries are evenly distributed through the mixture.

7. Fill a piping bag with the cheesecake mixture. Make sure to use a wide nozzle if not using a disposable piping bag. If using a disposable piping bag, cut the tip to create a 3cm (1¼in) hole.

8. Spoon half of the chocolate sponge batter into the prepared tin. Carefully pipe the cheesecake mixture in a ring in the middle of the chocolate batter. This will create a centre ring of cheesecake, so try to not let it touch the tin.

Recipe continues ...

9. Spoon the remaining half of the chocolate batter on top of the cheesecake mixture, carefully smoothing it down to completely cover the cheesecake mix.

10. Bake for approximately 1 hour or until the cake springs back when lightly touched, and a skewer comes out clean of batter when inserted. Allow the cake to cool and then carefully turn out of the tin.

11. In a small pan, melt the black cherry jam. Using a pastry brush, coat the cake in the melted jam.

✱ This cake could also be made with dried blackcurrants and blackcurrant jam.

Our customers love anything we sell that has malt in it. But being The Hummingbird Bakers we weren't happy with just a simple chocolate cake with malt frosting, so we added chocolate fudge sauce, a cream cheese malt frosting and crushed malt chocolates to decorate.

Chocolate Malt Cake

SERVES 10–12

FOR THE CHOCOLATE FUDGE SAUCE

30g (1oz) DARK CHOCOLATE (MINIMUM 70% COCOA SOLIDS), ROUGHLY CHOPPED

20g (¾oz) COCOA POWDER, SIFTED

¼ tsp SALT

100g (3½oz) GOLDEN SYRUP

25g (1oz) CASTER SUGAR

60ml (2fl oz) DOUBLE CREAM

FOR THE SPONGE

120g (4oz) UNSALTED BUTTER, SOFTENED

300g (10½oz) CASTER SUGAR

3 LARGE EGGS

115ml (4fl oz) BUTTERMILK

40ml (1½fl oz) SUNFLOWER OIL

1 tsp VANILLA EXTRACT

160g (5½oz) PLAIN FLOUR

70g (2½oz) COCOA POWDER, SIFTED

1½ tsp BAKING POWDER

1 tsp SALT

Ingredients continue ...

1. To make the chocolate fudge sauce, mix the chopped dark chocolate, cocoa powder and salt in a medium bowl. In a medium pan, bring the golden syrup, caster sugar and double cream to the boil.

2. Pour the hot liquid over the chocolate and cocoa powder. Let this sit for a minute, and then whisk by hand until the mixture is glossy and smooth. Set aside while making the sponge.

3. Preheat the oven to 170°C (325°F), Gas mark 3, and line the cake tins with baking parchment.

4. In a freestanding electric mixer with the paddle attachment or using a hand-held electric whisk, cream the butter and sugar together until light and fluffy. Add the eggs one at a time, mixing well and scraping down the bowl after each addition.

5. In a jug, mix together the buttermilk, oil and vanilla extract by hand.

6. With the mixer or whisk on a medium speed, pour in the buttermilk mixture in a slow, steady stream. Scrape down the sides of the bowl as you go. The mixture might split at this point, but don't worry as it will come back together. Add 3 tablespoons of the fudge sauce prepared earlier, and mix well until fully incorporated.

7. Sift the dry ingredients together in a medium bowl, then add these to the batter. With the mixer or whisk on a medium speed, mix well until all the ingredients are evenly incorporated and the batter is smooth.

8. Divide the batter evenly among the three prepared cake tins. Bake for approximately 30–35 minutes or until the sponge bounces back when lightly touched.

Recipe continues ...

FOR THE FROSTING

900g (2lb) ICING SUGAR, SIFTED

150g (5½oz) UNSALTED BUTTER, SOFTENED

300g (10½oz) FULL-FAT CREAM CHEESE
(SUCH AS PHILADELPHIA)

240ml (8½fl oz) DOUBLE CREAM

120g (4oz) MALT POWDER
(SUCH AS HORLICKS OR OVALTINE)

FOR THE DECORATION

70g (2½oz) MALT CHOCOLATES (SUCH AS MALTESERS,
ABOUT 2 SMALL BAGS), ROUGHLY CRUSHED, PLUS
EXTRA WHOLE ONES

EQUIPMENT

THREE 20cm (8in) DIAMETER LOOSE-BOTTOMED
SANDWICH TINS

9. Allow the sponges to cool slightly in the tins and then pour the fudge sauce over the top of each cake while they are still warm. If the sauce has become too stiff, re-melt it gently over a pan of simmering water, stirring until it has loosened up enough to pour. Allow the cakes to cool completely before removing from the tins.

10. Using the freestanding electric mixer with the paddle attachment or the hand-held electric whisk, make the frosting by gradually mixing the icing sugar and butter together on a low speed until combined, sandy in texture and there are no large lumps of butter. Add a little of the cream cheese to loosen the mixture and beat until smooth, then gradually mix in the remaining cream cheese. Once incorporated, turn the speed to high and beat until the frosting is light and fluffy.

11. In a separate bowl, whisk together the double cream and malt powder until thick and it forms soft peaks. This can be done by hand as it thickens very quickly. Fold the malt cream into the cream cheese frosting by hand.

12. Once the sponge layers feel cool to the touch, you can assemble the cake. Place the first layer on a plate or cake card and top with 3–4 tablespoons of frosting. Smooth the frosting out using a palette knife, adding a little more if needed. Sprinkle a light layer of the crushed malt chocolates over the frosting.

13. Sandwich the second layer on top, then add more frosting and malt chocolates, followed by the third layer of cake. Next frost the sides and top of the cake, covering it completely so that no sponge is showing.

14. Finally, decorate the top of the cake with a generous sprinkling of the remaining crushed malt chocolates, and decorate around the edge of the top of the cake with the whole malt chocolates if you like.

★ The frosting for this cake is very soft, so make sure it's kept nice and cool before you decorate the cake.

We think this indulgent cake will satisfy even the most passionate chocolate lovers. This is a wonderful recipe to make for a party or get-together as it will serve a good number of people and has the 'wow' factor. To achieve the line-effect on the side frosting use a serrated knife and go around the sides of the cake gently.

Mississippi Mud Cake

SERVES 10-12

FOR THE SPONGE
250g (9oz) UNSALTED BUTTER, SOFTENED
600g (1lb 5oz) CASTER SUGAR
3 LARGE EGGS
470g (1lb 1oz) PLAIN FLOUR
140g (5oz) COCOA POWDER
2 tsp BICARBONATE OF SODA
½ tsp SALT
375ml (13fl oz) BUTTERMILK
1 tsp VANILLA EXTRACT
375ml (13fl oz) BOILING WATER

FOR THE FROSTING
800g (1¾lb) ICING SUGAR, SIFTED
120g (4oz) COCOA POWDER, SIFTED, PLUS EXTRA FOR DUSTING
150g (5½oz) UNSALTED BUTTER, CUBED
600g (1lb 5oz) FULL-FAT CREAM CHEESE (SUCH AS PHILADELPHIA)

FOR THE DECORATION
40g (1½oz) DARK CHOCOLATE (MINIMUM 70% COCOA SOLIDS), SHAVED WITH A VEGETABLE PEELER

EQUIPMENT
THREE 20cm (8in) DIAMETER LOOSE-BOTTOMED SANDWICH TINS

1. Preheat the oven to 170°C (325°F), Gas mark 3, and line the cake tins with baking parchment.

2. First make the sponge. In a freestanding electric mixer with the paddle attachment or using a hand-held electric whisk, cream the butter and sugar together until light and fluffy. Add the eggs one at a time, mixing well and scraping down the sides of the bowl after each addition.

3. In a medium bowl, sift the flour, cocoa powder, bicarbonate of soda and salt together. Mix the buttermilk and vanilla extract in a jug. Add the dry ingredients to the creamed butter and sugar in three additions, alternating with the buttermilk mixture. Mix well on a medium speed. Slowly add the boiling water, mixing until combined.

4. Divide the batter evenly among the three prepared cake tins. Bake for approximately 35–45 minutes or until the sponge bounces back when lightly touched. Remove from the tins and allow the sponges to cool completely before frosting.

5. Using the freestanding electric mixer with the paddle attachment or the hand-held electric whisk, gradually mix the icing sugar, cocoa powder and butter together on a low speed until fully combined, sandy in texture and there are no large lumps of butter. Add a little cream cheese to loosen the mixture and beat until smooth, then add the remaining cream cheese and mix on a slow speed until incorporated. Turn the speed to high and beat the frosting until light and fluffy.

6. Once the sponge layers feel cool to the touch you can assemble the cake. Place the first layer on a plate or cake card and top with 3–4 tablespoons of frosting. Smooth out the frosting using a palette knife, adding a little more if needed. Sandwich the second layer on top, then add more frosting, followed by the third layer of cake.

7. Next frost the sides and top of the cake, covering it completely so that no sponge is showing. Finally, decorate the top of the cake with chocolate shavings and dust with cocoa powder.

An easy-to-make cake that works well as a dessert, perhaps served with a little soured cream. It's ideal for those avoiding wheat or gluten. This cake will be soft when removed from the oven and will firm up as it cools.

Flourless Chocolate Cake

SERVES 10

5 LARGE EGGS

290g (10½oz) CASTER SUGAR

125ml (4½fl oz) WATER

340g (12oz) DARK CHOCOLATE (MINIMUM 70% COCOA SOLIDS), CHOPPED

225g (8oz) UNSALTED BUTTER, CUBED

FOR THE DECORATION

ICING SUGAR AND/OR COCOA POWDER

EQUIPMENT

ONE 23cm (9in) DIAMETER SPRING-FORM CAKE TIN

1. Preheat the oven to 160°C (320°F), Gas mark 3, and line the tin with baking parchment.

2. In a freestanding electric mixer with the whisk attachment or using a hand-held electric whisk, beat together the eggs and 120g (4oz) of the caster sugar until light and fluffy. The mixture should quadruple in size — it will take about 10 minutes.

3. In a medium pan, mix the remaining sugar with the water. Heat to dissolve the sugar and make a light syrup. Remove the pan from the heat and add the chopped chocolate and butter. Stir to combine and melt the ingredients together. Allow to cool slightly.

4. Add the warm chocolate liquid to the egg mixture and mix to combine, but only for a short time — approximately 20 seconds.

5. Pour the cake batter into the prepared tin and place into a larger roasting tin. Put into the oven and then carefully fill the roasting tin with water to reach just under the rim of the cake tin, creating a water bath (bain-marie). This allows for an even bake of the cake.

6. Bake the cake for approximately 50 minutes or until set. Check by touching the cake gently: if it feels set but not firm, then it is done. Leave the cake to cool completely in the tin before turning it out and dusting with icing sugar and/or cocoa powder to serve. You can eat it immediately or let it set further in the fridge, if desired.

Very moist, very tangy, very fruity and very delicious – this is one of our favourite layer cakes. Raspberries work best with the cream cheese and lemon, but you could substitute with another red berry if you like.

Lemon Cake with Lemon Cream Cheese Frosting

SERVES 10-12

FOR THE SPONGE
110g (4oz) UNSALTED BUTTER, SOFTENED

380g (13oz) CASTER SUGAR

320g (11oz) PLAIN FLOUR

4 tsp BAKING POWDER

320ml (11fl oz) BUTTERMILK

ZEST OF 2 LEMONS

3 LARGE EGGS

80g (3oz) RASPBERRY JAM

FOR THE FROSTING
900g (2lb) ICING SUGAR, SIFTED, PLUS EXTRA FOR DUSTING

ZEST OF 1½ LEMONS

150g (5½oz) UNSALTED BUTTER, SOFTENED

375g (13oz) FULL-FAT CREAM CHEESE (SUCH AS PHILADELPHIA)

FOR THE DECORATION
GRATED ZEST OF 1 LEMON (OPTIONAL)

A FEW RASPBERRIES (OPTIONAL)

EQUIPMENT
THREE 20cm (8in) DIAMETER LOOSE-BOTTOMED SANDWICH TINS

1. Preheat the oven to 170°C (325°F), Gas mark 3, and line the cake tins with baking parchment.

2. In a freestanding electric mixer with the paddle attachment or using a hand-held electric whisk, mix the butter, sugar, flour and baking powder together until it forms a sandy consistency.

3. In a large jug, mix together the buttermilk, lemon zest and eggs.

4. With the mixer or whisk on a medium speed, gradually pour half of the liquid into the crumb mixture, scraping down the sides of the bowl from time to time. Mix thoroughly until the batter is thick and smooth, without lumps. Once all lumps are gone, add the rest of the liquid and mix until combined.

5. Divide the batter evenly amongst the three prepared tins. Bake the sponges for 20–30 minutes or until golden brown and the sponge bounces back when lightly touched. Remove from the tins and allow to cool completely before frosting.

6. Using the freestanding electric mixer with the paddle attachment or the hand-held electric whisk, gradually mix the icing sugar, lemon zest and butter together on a low speed until combined and there are no large lumps of butter. Add a little of the cream cheese to loosen and beat until smooth, then add the rest of the cream cheese and beat the frosting until it is light and fluffy.

7. Once the sponge layers feel cool to the touch, you can assemble the cake. Place the first layer on a plate or cake card and spread on a layer of raspberry jam. Top with 3–4 tablespoons of frosting. Smooth the frosting out using a palette knife, adding a little more if needed. Sandwich the second layer on top, then add more jam and frosting, followed by the third layer of cake. Next, frost the sides and top of the cake, covering it completely so that no sponge is showing. Finally, decorate the top of the cake with a few raspberries and a light sprinkling of icing sugar and lemon zest, if desired.

Our classic Red Velvet Cupcakes are still the most popular cakes in our bakeries even after all these years. We wondered how to create something new for this best-loved flavour and we came up with this stunning but simple roulade. Make sure you use the gel paste listed below and not 'natural' red liquid colourings as they won't produce the deep red colour.

Red Velvet Roulade

SERVES 8–10

FOR THE SPONGE

130g (4½oz) PLAIN FLOUR

2 tbsp COCOA POWDER

½ tsp BICARBONATE OF SODA

PINCH OF SALT

120ml (4fl oz) BUTTERMILK

1 tsp VANILLA EXTRACT

1 tsp WHITE WINE VINEGAR

120g (4oz) UNSALTED BUTTER, SOFTENED

150g (5½oz) CASTER SUGAR

1 LARGE EGG

1½ tbsp RED GEL PASTE COLOURING

30ml (1fl oz) WATER

Ingredients continue ...

1. Preheat the oven to 180°C (350°F), Gas mark 4, and line the Swiss roll tin with baking parchment.

2. Sift together the flour, cocoa powder, bicarbonate of soda and salt. In a jug, mix together the buttermilk, vanilla extract and white wine vinegar.

3. In a freestanding electric mixer with the paddle attachment or using a hand-held electric whisk, cream the butter and sugar together until light and fluffy. Add the egg and mix well. Scrape down the sides of the bowl.

4. With the mixer or whisk on a slow speed, add the dry ingredients gradually to the creamed butter and sugar, alternating with the buttermilk mixture. End with an addition of dry ingredients. Dissolve the red gel paste colouring in the water, making sure the paste is completely dissolved and there are no lumps of paste left in the water. Add the dissolved paste mixture to the batter, making sure the colouring is evenly mixed throughout.

5. Spoon the batter into the prepared tin and spread to the edges. Bake for approximately 25 minutes or until the sponge is set on the top and springs back when lightly touched. Remove the sponge from the oven and cover with a damp tea towel. Allow the sponge to cool a little.

6. While the sponge is cooling, make the filling. In the freestanding electric mixer with the paddle attachment or using the hand-held electric whisk, beat the cream cheese until it is smooth. With the mixer or whisk on a medium speed, pour in the melted white chocolate, mixing until it is incorporated in the cream cheese. Add the butter, mixing well. Add the icing sugar and beat just until the filling is smooth and fluffy.

Recipe continues ...

FOR THE FILLING

250g (9oz) FULL-FAT CREAM CHEESE
(SUCH AS PHILADELPHIA)

130g (4½oz) WHITE CHOCOLATE, MELTED (SEE PAGE 295)

50g (1¾oz) UNSALTED BUTTER, WELL SOFTENED

50g (1¾oz) ICING SUGAR, SIFTED, PLUS
EXTRA FOR DUSTING

EQUIPMENT

ONE 32 x 23 x 2cm (13 x 9 x ¾in) SWISS ROLL TIN

7. Dust a sheet of baking parchment or a clean tea towel with icing sugar. Loosen the edges of the cake and invert the sponge onto the parchment or tea towel.

8. Beginning at the narrow edge of the sponge, roll the sponge and the parchment or towel up together. Cool completely on a rack, seam-side down, for 10–15 minutes.

9. Once cooled, gently unroll the sponge and carefully peel the paper from the top of the sponge.

10. Spread the filling over the inside of the sponge roll. Re-roll the sponge without the parchment or tea towel. Dust with icing sugar and serve.

* If you are concerned about the sponge cracking as you roll it up, dampen the tea towel (if using) before turning the cake out onto it.

This deceptively impressive layer cake is actually simple to make and perfect for a birthday gift. This cake is different to the cupcake version on page 73 and uses mascarpone instead of milk in the frosting. You can use any freshly baked cookie you like, either shop-bought or home-made, but avoid white chocolate chip as they will make the recipe too sweet.

Cookies & Cream Cake

SERVES 10-12

FOR THE SPONGE

110g (4oz) UNSALTED BUTTER, SOFTENED

380g (13oz) CASTER SUGAR

320g (11oz) PLAIN FLOUR

4 tsp BAKING POWDER

1 tsp SALT

320ml (11fl oz) BUTTERMILK

3 LARGE EGGS

135g (5oz) FRESH COOKIES (FROM THE BAKERY SECTION IN THE SUPERMARKET - THESE CAN BE A FAVOURITE FLAVOUR, SUCH AS CHOC CHIP/ DOUBLE CHOCOLATE, BUT NOT WHITE CHOCOLATE CHIP COOKIES)

FOR THE FROSTING

1kg (2lb 3oz) ICING SUGAR, SIFTED

320g (11oz) UNSALTED BUTTER, SOFTENED

500g (1lb 2oz) MASCARPONE

2-3 FRESH COOKIES, CRUMBLED (SEE ABOVE)

EQUIPMENT

THREE 20cm (8in) DIAMETER LOOSE-BOTTOMED SANDWICH TINS

1. Preheat the oven to 170°C (325°F), Gas mark 3, and line the cake tins with baking parchment.

2. In a freestanding electric mixer with the paddle attachment or using a hand-held electric whisk, mix the butter, sugar and dry ingredients together until they form a sandy consistency with no large lumps of butter.

3. In a separate large jug, mix together the buttermilk and eggs by hand.

4. With the mixer or whisk on a medium speed, add the liquid to the butter and flour mixture in a slow, steady stream. Scrape down the sides of the bowl as you go. Mix again until the batter is even and smooth.

5. Crumble the cookies into rough pieces, not too big, and stir them through the batter by hand. Divide the batter evenly among the prepared cake tins.

6. Bake for 30–35 minutes or until golden brown and the sponge bounces back when lightly touched. Allow the cakes to cool completely before removing from the tins.

7. Using the freestanding electric mixer with the paddle attachment or the hand-held electric whisk, make the frosting by gradually mixing the icing sugar and butter together on a low speed until combined and there are no large lumps of butter. Add about one-third of the mascarpone and beat until combined and smooth, then gradually add the remaining mascarpone and mix until completely incorporated. Turn the mixer speed to high and beat the frosting until it is light and fluffy.

8. Once the sponge layers feel cool to the touch, you can assemble the cake. Place the first layer on a plate or cake card and top with 3–4 tablespoons of frosting. Smooth it out using a palette knife, adding a little more if needed. Sprinkle over a handful of cookie pieces.

9. Sandwich the second layer on top, then add more frosting and cookie pieces, followed by the third layer of cake. Next frost the sides and top of the cake, covering it completely so that no sponge is showing. Finally, decorate the top of the cake with any remaining cookie pieces.

Maple and walnuts are a traditional combination but, if you wish, you can use pecans instead for this crunchy and tasty cake. We have recommended a tin size below, but if the tin you have is slightly smaller the recipe will still work, just remember not to fill your tin more than two-thirds full.

Maple & Walnut Streusel Cake

SERVES 10-12

FOR THE STREUSEL

50g (1¾oz) SOFT LIGHT BROWN SUGAR

80g (3oz) PLAIN FLOUR

1½ tsp GROUND CINNAMON

45g (1½oz) UNSALTED BUTTER, CUBED, PLUS EXTRA FOR GREASING

80g (3oz) WALNUTS, CHOPPED, PLUS EXTRA TO DECORATE

FOR THE SPONGE

170g (6oz) UNSALTED BUTTER, SOFTENED

250g (9oz) CASTER SUGAR

3 LARGE EGGS

1½ tsp VANILLA EXTRACT

280g (10oz) SOURED CREAM

420g (15oz) PLAIN FLOUR

2 tsp BAKING POWDER

½ tsp BICARBONATE OF SODA

½ tsp SALT

100ml (3½ fl oz) MAPLE SYRUP, TO DRIZZLE

FOR THE GLAZE

170g (6oz) ICING SUGAR, SIFTED

4 tbsp MAPLE SYRUP

EQUIPMENT

ONE 25cm (10in) DIAMETER NON-STICK RING CAKE TIN

1. Preheat the oven to 170°C (325°F), Gas mark 3, then grease the cake tin with butter and dust with flour.

2. To make the streusel, place the brown sugar, flour and cinnamon together in a bowl. Add the butter and rub the mixture together using your fingertips until it forms a crumble. Add the chopped walnuts and stir through. Set aside.

3. In a freestanding electric mixer with the paddle attachment or using a hand-held electric whisk, cream together the butter and sugar for the sponge until light and fluffy. Add the eggs one at a time, mixing well and scraping down the sides of the bowl after each addition. Mix in the vanilla extract. Add the soured cream and mix well.

4. In a separate large bowl, sift together the flour, baking powder, bicarbonate of soda and salt. Add the dry ingredients to the batter, and mix thoroughly at a medium speed until smooth and even.

5. Sprinkle half the streusel mixture into the base of the prepared tin, and top with half of the cake batter. Sprinkle the remaining streusel mix on top of the batter and then top with the remaining batter.

6. Bake the cake for 50–60 minutes or until golden on top and when tested with a skewer it comes out clean of batter. While the cake is still warm, drizzle over the maple syrup. Allow the cake to cool in the tin.

7. Next make the glaze. In a medium bowl, mix together the icing sugar and maple syrup with 2 tablespoons of water to form a smooth, runny glaze.

8. Turn the cooled cake out onto a cooling rack, so that it is streusel-side up. Sit the rack over a deep baking tray and coat the top of the cake in the prepared maple glaze. It will run down the sides of the cake and any extra will collect in the baking tray and can then be re-used for a second layer if you wish. Sprinkle over some chopped walnuts. Once the glaze has begun to set, you can transfer the cake to a plate or cake card.

A favourite old-time home-baking recipe. Delicious eaten warm as a dessert with custard or cream or at room temperature as an afternoon treat.

Pineapple Upside-Down Cake

SERVES 8-10

200g (7oz) UNSALTED BUTTER, SOFTENED, PLUS EXTRA FOR GREASING

200g (7oz) CASTER SUGAR, PLUS 3 tbsp FOR SPRINKLING

4 LARGE EGGS

200g (7oz) PLAIN FLOUR, PLUS EXTRA FOR DUSTING

2 tsp BAKING POWDER

½ tsp BICARBONATE OF SODA

½ tsp SALT

90ml (3fl oz) PINEAPPLE JUICE (FROM THE TIN)

6 SLICES OF TINNED PINEAPPLE

EQUIPMENT

ONE 23cm (9in) DIAMETER CAKE TIN

1. Preheat the oven to 170°C (325°F), Gas mark 3, then grease the cake tin with butter and dust with flour.

2. In a freestanding electric mixer with the paddle attachment or using a hand-held electric whisk, cream the butter and sugar together until light and fluffy. Add the eggs one at a time, mixing well and scraping down the sides of the bowl after each addition.

3. In a separate bowl, sift together the flour, baking powder, bicarbonate of soda and salt. Add the dry ingredients to the butter mixture, mixing well to form a smooth batter. Add the pineapple juice and mix thoroughly.

4. Sprinkle the 3 tablespoons of caster sugar over the base of the prepared cake tin. Arrange the pineapple slices in a circular pattern around the edge of the tin, with one in the middle, pressing them down flat so that no batter can creep underneath. Pour the cake batter over the pineapple slices.

5. Bake the cake for 35–45 minutes or until the sponge is golden brown and bounces back when lightly touched. Allow the cake to cool slightly in the tin, then carefully turn out onto a plate.

We don't often use Brazil nuts in our recipes, but their more savoury flavour is perfect with the sweetness of banana. A good recipe for using up over-ripe bananas and you can substitute with another type of nut if you prefer, just make sure that the total weight is the same as called for in the recipe.

Banana & Brazil Nut Loaf

SERVES 8-10

100g (3½oz) BRAZIL NUTS, ROUGHLY CHOPPED

200g (7oz) UNSALTED BUTTER, PLUS EXTRA FOR GREASING

300g (10½oz) SOFT LIGHT BROWN SUGAR

4 EGGS

300g (10½oz) PLAIN FLOUR, PLUS EXTRA FOR DUSTING

½ tsp GROUND CINNAMON

½ tsp GROUND GINGER

¼ tsp GROUND CLOVES

2 tsp BAKING POWDER

3 RIPE MEDIUM BANANAS

EQUIPMENT

ONE 900g (2lb) LOAF TIN

1. Preheat the oven to 170°C (325°F), Gas mark 3, then grease the loaf tin with butter and dust with flour.

2. Spread the chopped Brazil nuts evenly over a baking tray. Toast the nuts in the oven for 5–10 minutes, checking often as they will colour quickly. Once toasted, remove and set aside to cool completely. Leave the oven turned on.

3. In a freestanding electric mixer with the paddle attachment or using a hand-held electric whisk, cream the butter and sugar together until light and fluffy. Add the eggs one at a time, mixing well and scraping down the sides of the bowl after each addition.

4. In a medium bowl, mix together the dry ingredients and 60g (2oz) of the toasted nuts. Add the dry ingredients to the butter and egg mixture. Mix on a medium speed, making sure the ingredients are well incorporated.

5. Mash the bananas in a bowl using a fork, then add to the batter and mix well.

6. Pour the batter into the prepared loaf tin. Sprinkle the remaining toasted nuts over the top of the raw loaf.

7. Bake for approximately 1–1¼ hours or until a skewer inserted into the centre comes out clean. If the top of the loaf is browning too quickly, cover with foil and continue to bake. Allow the loaf to cool a little before turning it out of the tin onto a wire rack to cool completely, then cut into slices to serve.

We invented this more-than-fudge cake at the bakery. We weren't sure what to call it, so we decided to name it after one of our favourite cities: the Windy City — Chicago.

Chicago Fudge Cake

SERVES 10–12

FOR THE FUDGE

55g (2oz) UNSALTED BUTTER

180g (6½oz) CASTER SUGAR

90g (3oz) SOFT LIGHT BROWN SUGAR

125ml (4½fl oz) DOUBLE CREAM

¼ tsp VANILLA EXTRACT

FOR THE FROSTING

725ml (1 pint 5fl oz) DOUBLE CREAM

1 tbsp VANILLA EXTRACT

170g (6oz) UNSALTED BUTTER

60g (2oz) GOLDEN SYRUP

450g (1lb) DARK CHOCOLATE (MINIMUM 70% COCOA SOLIDS), CHOPPED

FOR THE SPONGE

110g (4oz) COCOA POWDER, SIFTED

2 tbsp INSTANT COFFEE MIXED WITH 240ml (8½fl oz) BOILING WATER OR 240ml (8½fl oz) ESPRESSO COFFEE (IF YOU HAVE A MACHINE)

125g (4½oz) SOURED CREAM

1½ tsp VANILLA EXTRACT

210g (7½oz) PLAIN FLOUR

½ tsp BAKING POWDER

¾ tsp BICARBONATE OF SODA

225g (8oz) UNSALTED BUTTER, SOFTENED

340g (12oz) CASTER SUGAR

2 LARGE EGGS

Ingredients continue ...

1. Preheat the oven to 170°C (325°F), Gas mark 3, and line the cake tins with baking parchment.

2. To make the fudge, line a baking tray with baking parchment. Mix the butter, caster sugar, light brown sugar, cream and vanilla extract in a medium pan. Cook over a medium heat, stirring constantly, until the sugar dissolves. Then cook over a low heat, without stirring, until the sugar reaches the hard crack stage (when a drop of boiling syrup immersed in cold water cracks) — about 150°C (302°F) on a sugar thermometer.

3. Remove the pan from the heat and carefully pour the syrup onto the prepared tray. Allow to cool completely.

4. When cool, break the fudge into rough small pieces. Set aside.

5. To make the frosting, mix the double cream, vanilla extract, butter and golden syrup in a medium pan and bring to a gentle simmer over a low heat. Remove from the heat.

6. Place the chopped dark chocolate in a large mixing bowl. Pour the hot cream mixture onto the chocolate, stirring until all the chocolate has melted and is smooth. Cover with cling film and refrigerate for a couple of hours until set but still soft enough to spread.

7. In a medium bowl, mix the cocoa powder and hot coffee together well with a whisk to ensure the cocoa powder is fully dissolved in the coffee. Allow to cool.

8. In a jug, mix the cooled coffee mixture, soured cream and vanilla extract together. In a medium bowl, sift the flour, baking powder and bicarbonate of soda together.

Recipe continues ...

EQUIPMENT

THREE 20cm (8in) DIAMETER LOOSE-BOTTOMED
SANDWICH TINS

SUGAR THERMOMETER

9. In a freestanding electric mixer with the paddle attachment or using a hand-held electric whisk, cream the butter and sugar together until light and fluffy. Add the eggs one at a time, mixing well and scraping down the bowl after each addition.

10. On a slow speed, add the dry ingredients, alternating with the soured cream mixture. Mix until the batter is smooth and glossy.

11. Divide the batter evenly among the three prepared cake tins and bake for 30–35 minutes or until the sponge bounces back when lightly touched. Allow to cool completely in the tins before frosting.

12. Once the sponge layers feel cool to the touch, you can assemble the cake. Place the first layer on a plate or cake card and top with 3–4 tablespoons of frosting. Smooth the frosting out using a palette knife, adding a little more if needed. Sprinkle a handful of the fudge pieces over the frosting. Sandwich the second layer on top, then add more frosting and fudge pieces, followed by the third layer of cake.

13. Next frost the sides and top of the cake, covering it completely so that no sponge is showing. Finally, decorate the top of the cake with the remaining fudge pieces.

* See the pictures opposite for tips on how to frost your cake.

We're all about roulades lately — they are really easy, tasty and always look impressive — so our favourite pumpkin and cream cheese combination gets the roly-poly makeover.

Pumpkin & Cream Cheese Roulade

SERVES 8-10

FOR THE SPONGE

120g (4oz) PLAIN FLOUR

2 tsp GROUND CINNAMON

1 tsp BICARBONATE OF SODA

3 EGGS

200g (7oz) CASTER SUGAR

120g (4oz) TINNED PUMPKIN PURÉE

ICING SUGAR, FOR DUSTING

FOR THE FILLING

170g (6oz) ICING SUGAR, SIFTED

60g (2oz) UNSALTED BUTTER, SOFTENED

240g (8½oz) FULL-FAT CREAM CHEESE (SUCH AS PHILADELPHIA)

½ tsp VANILLA EXTRACT

EQUIPMENT

ONE 32 x 23 x 2cm (13 x 9 x ¾in) SWISS ROLL TIN

1. Preheat the oven to 170°C (325°F), Gas mark 3, and line the Swiss roll tin with baking parchment.

2. First make the sponge. Sift the flour, cinnamon and bicarbonate of soda together and set aside. In a freestanding electric mixer with the whisk attachment or using a hand-held electric whisk, whisk the eggs and sugar together until pale, fluffy and doubled in volume. Fold the pumpkin purée into the mixture, then fold in the sifted dry ingredients.

3. Pour the batter into the prepared tin. Bake for approximately 15 minutes or until the sponge bounces back when touched lightly. Allow to cool in the tin.

4. Using the freestanding electric mixer with the paddle attachment or the hand-held electric whisk, gradually mix the icing sugar and butter together on a low speed until it forms a sandy consistency.

5. Add a little of the cream cheese to loosen the mixture and beat until smooth, then add the rest of the cream cheese and mix on a slow speed until incorporated. Mix through the vanilla extract. Turn up the speed of the mixer or whisk and beat the filling until it is light and fluffy.

6. Dust a clean tea towel with icing sugar. Loosen the edges of the cake and invert the sponge onto the tea towel.

7. Beginning at the narrow edge of the sponge, roll the sponge and the towel up together. Cool on a rack, seam side down, for 10–15 minutes.

8. Once cooled, gently unroll and carefully peel the paper from the top of the sponge. Spread the cream cheese filling over the inside of the sponge roll. Re-roll the sponge without the tea towel and dust with icing sugar just before serving.

* See page 110 for step-by-step photographs showing how best to roll up a roulade. You can use either baking parchment or a clean tea towel.

* If you are concerned about the sponge cracking as you roll it up, dampen the tea towel (if using) before turning the cake out onto it.

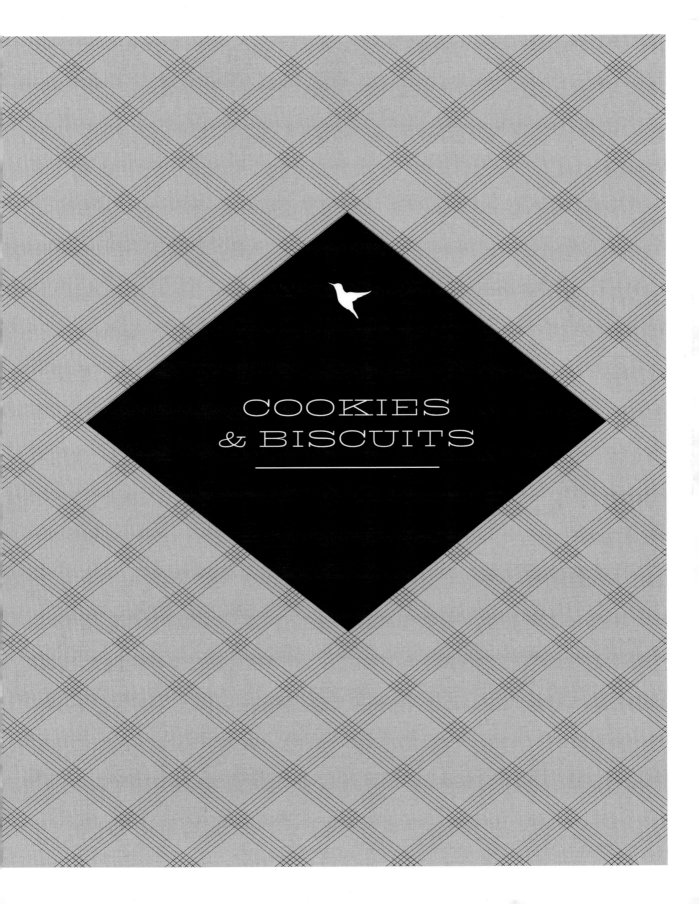

COOKIES
& BISCUITS

No American bakery would be complete without its own version of classic Linzer Cookies or Linzer Torte. Originating from Austria, a traditional torte consists of a pastry case made with ground almonds, flour, spices and egg, filled with jam and topped with a pastry lattice — a little like a Bakewell Tart. Here's our cookie version.

Linzer Cookies

MAKES 20–25 COOKIES

280g (10oz) UNSALTED BUTTER, SOFTENED
150g (5½oz) CASTER SUGAR
380g (13oz) PLAIN FLOUR, PLUS EXTRA FOR DUSTING
½ tsp GROUND CINNAMON
60g (2oz) GROUND ALMONDS
200g (7oz) SEEDLESS STRAWBERRY JAM

EQUIPMENT
TWO HEART-SHAPED CUTTERS, ONE 8cm (3in) AT ITS WIDEST POINT, AND ONE 5cm (2in) WIDE

1. Line three to four baking trays with baking parchment.

2. Using a hand-held electric whisk or a freestanding electric mixer with the paddle attachment, cream the butter and caster sugar together until light and fluffy. In a medium bowl, sift together the flour and cinnamon and mix in the ground almonds. Add the dry ingredients to the creamed butter and sugar and mix at a medium speed until a dough forms.

3. Turn the dough out onto a lightly floured surface and bring it together with your hands. Divide the dough into two balls, press to flatten them a little, wrap in cling film and place in the fridge to rest for about 30 minutes.

4. Once the dough has rested, roll out each piece between same-sized sheets of baking parchment that have been lightly dusted with flour. The dough should be about 4mm (⅛in) thick. Keep the dough between the baking parchment and place each piece on a chopping board, then leave to rest in the fridge again, for about 15 minutes.

5. Preheat the oven to 170°C (325°F), Gas mark 3. Once the dough is rested, remove the top sheet of paper from each piece. Using the larger cutter cut out cookies and place them on the prepared baking trays.

6. Use the smaller cutter to cut the centres out of half of the cookies to create a cookie top with a heart-shaped hole. More cookies and cookie tops can be made with any leftover dough.

7. Bake for approximately 15 minutes or until they are a light golden colour. Set aside to cool.

8. In a small pan, heat up the strawberry jam, bringing it to a gentle simmer. Remove from the heat and allow to cool slightly. Spoon about ½ teaspoon of jam onto each cookie bottom, then place a cookie top on each to create a sandwich.

We know macaroons are not usually found in the American baking repertoire, but we couldn't help putting these yummy French crunchy-chewy biscuits into a home-baking cookbook.

Hazelnut & Chocolate Macaroons

MAKES 16–18 MACAROONS

FOR THE MACAROONS

340g (12oz) ICING SUGAR, SIFTED

110g (4oz) HAZELNUTS, TOASTED AND PEELED

3 tbsp COCOA POWDER, SIFTED

3 LARGE EGG WHITES

PINCH OF SALT

FOR THE FILLING

125ml (4½fl oz) DOUBLE CREAM

110g (4oz) DARK CHOCOLATE CHIPS
(MINIMUM 70% COCOA SOLIDS)

EQUIPMENT

LARGE PIPING BAG WITH A 1½cm (⅔in) ROUND NOZZLE

1. Line two to three baking trays with baking parchment.

2. Into a food processor, put 140g (5oz) of the icing sugar along with the hazelnuts and cocoa powder, and process until they are very fine. Sift and discard any larger pieces of nut.

3. Using a hand-held electric whisk or a freestanding electric mixer with the whisk attachment, whip up the egg whites and salt until they form stiff peaks. Gradually add the remaining icing sugar, a tablespoon at a time, with the mixer or whisk on a medium speed — this will take up to 3 minutes. Scrape down the sides of the bowl as you go.

4. Once all the sugar is added, beat until the meringue is glossy — approximately 30 more seconds.

5. Carefully fold the nut mixture into the meringue using a rubber spatula. Transfer the mixture into the piping bag.

6. Pipe roughly 32 discs onto the prepared trays, each about 5cm (2in) wide and spaced evenly apart. Bang the trays carefully on a table to knock any large air bubbles out of the macaroons. Using the tip of your finger and a little water, press down any peaks made by the piping process. Allow the macaroons to air-dry for 30 minutes before baking.

7. Preheat the oven to 160°C (320°F), Gas mark 3. Bake the macaroons for 15 minutes. Be careful not to overcook them or they will crack. Allow to cool slightly for 5 minutes and then carefully peel from the paper and allow to cool completely.

8. To make the filling, heat the cream in a small pan until just boiling. Place the chocolate chips in a medium bowl. Pour the very hot cream over the chocolate, and stir until the chocolate is completely melted and smooth. Set aside to thicken.

9. Once the ganache has thickened and the macaroons are cool, spread about 1 teaspoon of the filling onto a macaroon and sandwich two together.

These mini cookies make perfect gifts when put into little clear bags and tied with a ribbon. Or you can just eat straight away with a cup of milky tea!

Chocolate Truffle Cookies

MAKES 12–14 COOKIES

80g (3oz) PLAIN FLOUR

25g (1oz) COCOA POWDER

½ tsp BAKING POWDER

90g (3oz) CASTER SUGAR

25g (1oz) UNSALTED BUTTER, CUBED

1 EGG

10ml (½fl oz) AMARETTO

50g (1¾oz) ICING SUGAR, TO COAT

1. Line two or three baking trays with baking parchment.

2. Sift the flour, cocoa and baking powder into a medium mixing bowl. Stir in the sugar. Using your fingertips, rub the butter into the dry ingredients until the mixture forms a sandy consistency with no large lumps of butter.

3. In a jug, mix the egg and amaretto together. Stir this liquid into the butter and dry ingredients. Mix to form a dough. The mixture may seem very dry at first, but keep mixing and it will come together. Wrap the dough in cling film and chill in the fridge for approximately 30–40 minutes.

4. Preheat the oven to 180°C (350°F), Gas mark 4. Place the icing sugar in a bowl. Make walnut-sized balls of the dough, each about 3½cm (1½in) in diameter, and toss in the sugar so that they are completely coated.

5. Place the balls onto the prepared baking trays and bake for 10–12 minutes. Allow to cool completely before serving.

These easy-peasy thumbprint cookies are perfect when served after a meal as a home-made version of a petit four. They do firm up once they've cooled, so be careful not to overbake.

Mint Chocolate Thumbprint Cookies

MAKES 20–24 COOKIES

FOR THE COOKIES

60g (2oz) DARK CHOCOLATE (MINIMUM 70% COCOA SOLIDS), ROUGHLY CHOPPED

110g (4oz) UNSALTED BUTTER, SOFTENED

40g (1½oz) CASTER SUGAR

1 tbsp SOFT DARK BROWN SUGAR

1 LARGE EGG YOLK

½ tsp VANILLA EXTRACT

1 tsp PEPPERMINT ESSENCE

125g (4½oz) PLAIN FLOUR

30g (1oz) COCOA POWDER

¼ tsp SALT

75g (2½oz) DEMERARA SUGAR

FOR THE FILLING

40g (1½oz) WHITE CHOCOLATE, ROUGHLY CHOPPED

1½ tbsp DOUBLE CREAM

1 tsp PEPPERMINT ESSENCE

EQUIPMENT

PIPING BAG (OPTIONAL)

1. In a microwave-safe bowl, carefully melt the dark chocolate in the microwave, or alternatively do this in a heatproof bowl set over a pan of simmering water. Check and stir regularly during melting.

2. In a freestanding electric mixer with the paddle attachment or using a hand-held electric whisk, cream the butter and two sugars together until light and fluffy. Add the egg yolk, vanilla extract and peppermint essence. Mix well, scraping down the sides of the bowl as you go.

3. Add the melted chocolate and mix thoroughly. Sift in the flour, cocoa and salt and mix to form a smooth cookie dough. Wrap the dough in cling film and place in the fridge to set for approximately 40 minutes.

4. Preheat the oven to 170°C (325°F), Gas mark 3, and line two to three baking trays with baking parchment.

5. Once rested, roll tablespoon-sized amounts of the dough into balls. Roll the dough balls in the demerara sugar, completely coating them in sugar.

6. Place the dough balls onto the prepared baking trays, spacing them evenly apart. Using your thumb, make an indent into the middle of each ball. Bake the cookies for approximately 15 minutes or until they are slightly firm and cracked around the outside. Allow to cool slightly.

7. While the cookies are cooling, make the filling. Place the white chocolate into a heatproof bowl. Heat up the double cream to boiling in the microwave or a very small pan. Pour the very hot cream over the white chocolate and then leave it to melt. Don't stir at this stage as it might split.

8. Once the chocolate has melted, add the peppermint essence and whisk until smooth.

9. Fill the indents in the cookies with the minty chocolate filling. You can use a teaspoon or a piping bag. Place the cookies in the fridge for about 30 minutes to allow the filling to set.

Shortcakes are wonderfully soft, spongy American cakes that look like scones. Enjoy them as the classic base to a berry shortcake — serve with strawberries or any other berry or soft fruit and either whipped cream or thick custard.

Basic Shortcakes

MAKES 8 SHORTCAKES

340g (12oz) PLAIN FLOUR, PLUS EXTRA FOR DUSTING

1 tbsp BAKING POWDER

½ tsp SALT

120g (4oz) COLD UNSALTED BUTTER, CUBED

160ml (5½fl oz) WHOLE MILK, PLUS EXTRA FOR BRUSHING

3 tbsp CASTER SUGAR, FOR SPRINKLING

EQUIPMENT

ONE 7.5cm (3in) ROUND COOKIE CUTTER

1. Preheat the oven to 180°C (350°F), Gas mark 4. Line a baking tray with baking parchment.

2. In a large bowl, sift together the flour, baking powder and salt. Add the butter and, using your fingertips, rub it into the dry ingredients until it forms a crumb-like consistency with no large lumps of butter.

3. Make a well in the centre and pour in the milk. Mix the ingredients together with a spoon until they come together to form a dough — be careful not to overmix the dough.

4. Turn the dough out onto a lightly floured surface and fold it over itself a couple of times until it holds together. Pat out the dough to about 2cm (¾in) thick. Using the cutter, cut out eight shortcakes. If reusing the offcuts, try not to overwork or handle the dough too much when reshaping.

5. Place the shortcakes on the prepared tray. Brush the tops with a small amount of whole milk and sprinkle each with a teaspoon of caster sugar. Bake for approximately 15 minutes or until they have risen and are a golden brown colour.

A little Italian-themed, quick and easy-to-bake cookie. These can be made with orange instead, but won't be as tangy. Make sure you don't overbake them.

Lemon & Ricotta Cookies

MAKES 18-20 COOKIES

FOR THE COOKIES
210g (7½oz) PLAIN FLOUR
½ tsp BAKING POWDER
½ tsp SALT
60g (2oz) UNSALTED BUTTER, SOFTENED
200g (7oz) CASTER SUGAR
1 EGG
100g (3½oz) RICOTTA CHEESE
1½ tbsp LEMON JUICE
GRATED ZEST OF 1 LEMON

FOR THE GLAZE
120g (4oz) ICING SUGAR
1½ tbsp LEMON JUICE
GRATED ZEST OF 1 LEMON

1. Preheat the oven to 170°C (325°F), Gas mark 3, and line two to three baking trays with baking parchment.

2. Sift together the flour, baking powder and salt. Using a hand-held electric whisk or a freestanding electric mixer with the paddle attachment, cream the butter and caster sugar together until light and fluffy. Add the egg and mix well. Scrape down the sides of the bowl as you go.

3. Add the ricotta cheese, lemon juice and lemon zest. Mix until all the ingredients are incorporated. Add the dry ingredients and mix on a slow speed until combined.

4. Spoon the dough onto the prepared baking trays, about 2 tablespoons per cookie. Bake for approximately 15 minutes or until golden brown in colour. Allow to cool.

5. To make the glaze, put the icing sugar, lemon juice and zest in a medium bowl and mix together until smooth. Spoon about ½ teaspoon of glaze onto the top of each cookie. Use the back of the teaspoon to spread the glaze. Allow the glaze to set and harden before serving.

A good old PB&J sandwich … but in cookie form! Leaving the dough for a few hours in the fridge before baking will make it much easier to slice into cookies.

Peanut Butter & Jam Pinwheel Cookies

MAKES 16–20 COOKIES

60g (2oz) SMOOTH RASPBERRY JAM

1 tsp CORNFLOUR

100g (3½oz) UNSALTED BUTTER, SOFTENED

100g (3½oz) SMOOTH PEANUT BUTTER

180g (6½oz) CASTER SUGAR

1 LARGE EGG

2 tbsp WHOLE MILK

340g (12oz) PLAIN FLOUR

½ tsp BICARBONATE OF SODA

¼ tsp SALT

1. Get ready two pieces of baking parchment, each about 38 x 25cm (15 x 10in).

2. In a small bowl, mix the raspberry jam and cornflour together until smooth and the cornflour has dissolved.

3. In a freestanding electric mixer with the paddle attachment or using a hand-held electric whisk, cream the butter, peanut butter and the sugar together until light and fluffy. Add the egg and milk. Scrape down the sides of the bowl every now and then.

4. Sift in the flour, bicarbonate of soda and salt, mixing on a slow speed until well incorporated and the mixture forms a dough.

5. Place the dough on one of the prepared pieces of baking parchment. Press the dough out slightly using your hands, then top with the second sheet of baking parchment. Gently roll the dough out to reach the edges of the paper. Remove the top sheet of baking parchment and spread the jam evenly over the dough, leaving about 1cm (½in) around the edge.

6. Carefully loosen the edge of the dough on the long side of the paper. Using the edge of the paper as a 'handle', roll the dough up Swiss-roll style, making sure to seal the seam and keeping it on the underside of the roll. Wrap the roll in cling film. Place the roll in the fridge and allow to set for a couple of hours, preferably overnight.

7. Preheat the oven to 170°C (325°F), Gas mark 3, and line two to three baking trays with baking parchment. Once set, slice the roll into 2cm (¾in) thick slices.

8. Place the slices on the prepared baking trays, about 5cm (2in) apart. Bake for approximately 10–12 minutes or until golden brown. Allow to cool completely before serving.

Another thumbprint cookie recipe to try out (see also the recipe on page 134). Keep them in a biscuit tin and enjoy as a small afternoon treat or pop into a lunchbox. These will harden as they cool down, so make sure you don't overbake.

Pecan & Toffee Thumbprint Cookies

MAKES 16–18 COOKIES

110g (4oz) FULL-FAT CREAM CHEESE (SUCH AS PHILADELPHIA)

70g (2½oz) UNSALTED BUTTER, SOFTENED

80g (3oz) ICING SUGAR, SIFTED

¼ tsp VANILLA EXTRACT

200g (7oz) PLAIN FLOUR

¼ tsp BICARBONATE OF SODA

50g (1¾oz) PECAN NUTS, FINELY CHOPPED

10 TOFFEE SWEETS, CUT IN HALF

1. Line two baking trays with baking parchment.

2. Using a hand-held electric whisk or a freestanding electric mixer with the paddle attachment, beat the cream cheese, butter, icing sugar and vanilla extract together until fluffy. With the mixer or whisk on a slow speed, sift in the flour and bicarbonate of soda, mixing well to incorporate all the ingredients.

3. Add the chopped pecan nuts, mixing well to make sure they are evenly dispersed through the dough. Place the dough in the fridge to chill for 30 minutes.

4. Preheat the oven to 180°C (350°F), Gas mark 4. Roll the chilled dough into 4cm (1½in) size balls. Place the dough balls onto the prepared baking sheets, spacing them evenly apart.

5. Using your thumb, make a deep indent in the centre of each dough ball. Place half a toffee sweet in each indent. Bake the cookies for 14–16 minutes or until they are golden brown and cooked through.

We love peanut butter as a filling for these chocolate shortcakes, but if you want to use another filling, try some blackcurrant jam and thick cream instead. It's important to chill the dough in the freezer so that it has time to firm up before baking.

Chocolate Shortcakes with a Peanut Butter Filling

MAKES 6 SHORTCAKES

FOR THE SHORTCAKES

340g (12oz) PLAIN FLOUR, PLUS EXTRA FOR DUSTING

2 tbsp COCOA POWDER

¾ tsp BAKING POWDER

¼ tsp SALT

80g (3oz) CASTER SUGAR

65g (2oz) UNSALTED BUTTER, CUBED

85g (3oz) MILK CHOCOLATE CHIPS

60ml (2fl oz) DOUBLE CREAM

1 tsp VANILLA EXTRACT

3 LARGE EGGS

30g (1oz) DEMERARA SUGAR

FOR THE FILLING

280g (10oz) FULL-FAT CREAM CHEESE (SUCH AS PHILADELPHIA)

60g (2oz) CRUNCHY PEANUT BUTTER

60g (2oz) ICING SUGAR, SIFTED

EQUIPMENT

6cm (2½in) ROUND COOKIE CUTTER

1. Line a baking tray with baking parchment.

2. Sift the flour, cocoa powder, baking powder and salt together into a large mixing bowl and mix in the caster sugar. Using your fingertips, rub the butter into the dry ingredients until it reaches a sandy consistency. Add the chocolate chips and mix through.

3. In a jug, mix the double cream, vanilla extract and two of the eggs together. Pour this into the flour mixture and stir until it forms a rough dough (there will still be some dry bits).

4. Turn the dough out onto a lightly floured surface and pat down until it is 4cm (1½in) thick. Cut out six discs using the cookie cutter. Make an extra cake with any remaining dough.

5. Place the shortcakes onto the prepared baking tray, and put in the freezer to chill for about 20 minutes. (This step is important, but don't freeze for more than 20 minutes as the dough won't cook from frozen.)

6. Preheat the oven to 170°C (325°F), Gas mark 3. In a small bowl, beat the remaining egg with a fork. Brush the tops of the shortcakes with beaten egg and sprinkle with the demerara sugar.

7. Bake for 20–25 minutes or until firm. Allow to cool completely before slicing and filling.

8. To make the filling, use a freestanding electric mixer with the paddle attachment or a hand-held electric whisk to beat the cream cheese and peanut butter together until smooth. Add the icing sugar and mix thoroughly until the filling is smooth and fluffy.

9. Cut the shortcakes in half and place on a tray or plate. Spoon 2–3 tablespoons of filling onto six halves. With the back of the spoon, spread the filling slightly and then sandwich two halves together.

These have a lovely crunch that will increase the longer you bake them. If you prefer them to still have a bit of chew, then decrease the baking time slightly.

Syrup Crunchie Cookies

MAKES 20 COOKIES

250g (9oz) UNSALTED BUTTER

220ml (8fl oz) SWEETENED CONDENSED MILK

180g (6½oz) GOLDEN SYRUP

1 tsp VANILLA EXTRACT

180g (6½oz) CORN FLAKES

250g (9oz) PLAIN FLOUR

90g (3oz) CUSTARD POWDER

2 tsp BICARBONATE OF SODA

180g (6½oz) PORRIDGE OATS

30g (1oz) DEMERARA SUGAR, FOR SPRINKLING

1. Preheat the oven to 160°C (320°F), Gas mark 3, and line two to three baking trays with baking parchment.

2. In a medium saucepan, gently heat the butter, condensed milk, golden syrup and vanilla extract until the butter has melted.

3. In a large bowl, roughly crush up the corn flakes into smaller pieces. Sift the flour, custard powder and bicarbonate of soda into the corn flakes, then mix in the oats, making sure all of the ingredients are well combined. Pour the melted liquid into the dry ingredients and mix with a spoon until well incorporated.

4. Spoon the cookie mixture onto the prepared baking trays — about 2 generous tablespoons per cookie. Using an ice-cream scoop makes this easy. Space the cookies evenly apart as they do spread slightly.

5. Flatten the tops of the cookies with your fingers and sprinkle each cookie generously with demerara sugar.

6. Bake the cookies for 10–15 minutes or until golden brown. Allow to cool before removing from the baking trays.

These are more chocolaty than our original peanut butter cookies and use a firmer dough. If you prefer, you can roll the dough into a large sausage shape and slice into rounds.

Peanut Butter & Chocolate Cookies

MAKES 20–30 COOKIES

170g (6oz) PLAIN FLOUR

40g (1½oz) COCOA POWDER

½ tsp BICARBONATE OF SODA

PINCH OF SALT

115g (4oz) UNSALTED BUTTER, SOFTENED

120g (4oz) CRUNCHY PEANUT BUTTER

120g (4oz) CASTER SUGAR, PLUS 40g (1½oz) EXTRA FOR ROLLING

90g (3oz) SOFT LIGHT BROWN SUGAR

1 LARGE EGG

1 tsp VANILLA EXTRACT

1. Preheat the oven to 170°C (325°F), Gas mark 3, and line two to three baking trays with baking parchment.

2. Sift together the flour, cocoa powder, bicarbonate of soda and salt.

3. Using a hand-held electric whisk or a freestanding electric mixer with the paddle attachment, cream the butter, peanut butter and both sugars until light and fluffy. Add the egg and mix well, scraping down the sides of the bowl as you go. With the speed on slow, add the dry ingredients and mix until combined and a dough is formed.

4. Put the extra caster sugar in a small bowl. Roll the dough into 4–5cm (1½–2in) balls, and roll each ball in the caster sugar to coat. Place the dough balls onto the prepared baking trays, keeping them about 4cm (1½in) apart.

5. Bake for 10–15 minutes or until the cookies have a crusty surface and have cracked. Cool completely before serving.

These have a lovely crunch that will increase the longer you bake them. If you prefer them to still have a bit of chew, then decrease the baking time slightly.

Syrup Crunchie Cookies

MAKES 20 COOKIES

250g (9oz) UNSALTED BUTTER

220ml (8fl oz) SWEETENED CONDENSED MILK

180g (6½oz) GOLDEN SYRUP

1 tsp VANILLA EXTRACT

180g (6½oz) CORN FLAKES

250g (9oz) PLAIN FLOUR

90g (3oz) CUSTARD POWDER

2 tsp BICARBONATE OF SODA

180g (6½oz) PORRIDGE OATS

30g (1oz) DEMERARA SUGAR, FOR SPRINKLING

1. Preheat the oven to 160°C (320°F), Gas mark 3, and line two to three baking trays with baking parchment.

2. In a medium saucepan, gently heat the butter, condensed milk, golden syrup and vanilla extract until the butter has melted.

3. In a large bowl, roughly crush up the corn flakes into smaller pieces. Sift the flour, custard powder and bicarbonate of soda into the corn flakes, then mix in the oats, making sure all of the ingredients are well combined. Pour the melted liquid into the dry ingredients and mix with a spoon until well incorporated.

4. Spoon the cookie mixture onto the prepared baking trays — about 2 generous tablespoons per cookie. Using an ice-cream scoop makes this easy. Space the cookies evenly apart as they do spread slightly.

5. Flatten the tops of the cookies with your fingers and sprinkle each cookie generously with demerara sugar.

6. Bake the cookies for 10–15 minutes or until golden brown. Allow to cool before removing from the baking trays.

A wonderful store-cupboard cookie recipe, we've added some malt powder to make these cookies even tastier. As with all our cookie recipes, the longer you bake, the crunchier and less chewy they'll be — it's a matter of personal preference.

Corn Flake Cookies

MAKES 18–22 COOKIES

FOR THE CORN FLAKES

80g (3oz) CORN FLAKES

20g (¾oz) MALT POWDER (SUCH AS HORLICKS OR OVALTINE)

20g (¾oz) CASTER SUGAR

½ tsp SALT

50g (1¾oz) UNSALTED BUTTER, MELTED

FOR THE DOUGH

225g (8oz) UNSALTED BUTTER, SOFTENED

350g (12oz) SOFT LIGHT BROWN SUGAR

2 LARGE EGGS

½ tsp VANILLA EXTRACT

400g (14oz) PLAIN FLOUR

½ tsp SALT

1 tsp BAKING POWDER

1 tsp BICARBONATE OF SODA

200g (7oz) DARK CHOCOLATE CHIPS (MINIMUM 70% COCOA SOLIDS)

1. Preheat the oven to 170°C (325°F), Gas mark 3. Line three to four baking trays with baking parchment.

2. In a medium bowl, roughly crush up the corn flakes into smaller pieces. Add the malt powder, sugar and salt to the corn flakes and mix well. Pour the melted butter over the corn flake mix, and stir to evenly coat the dry ingredients in butter.

3. Spread the corn flake mix onto one of the prepared baking trays. Bake for 10–15 minutes or until the corn flakes are crispy. Set aside to cool, leaving the oven turned on at the same temperature.

4. Using a hand-held electric whisk or a freestanding electric mixer with the paddle attachment, cream the butter and light brown sugar together until light and fluffy. Add the eggs one at a time, mixing well after each addition. Add the vanilla extract and mix through.

5. Sift in the flour, salt, baking powder and bicarbonate of soda. Mix well on a slow speed to form a cookie dough. Add the chocolate chips and the cooled corn flake mixture to the cookie dough and mix well to evenly incorporate.

6. Scoop the cookie dough into even-sized balls, each about two heaped tablespoons, and arrange on the prepared baking trays. Space the cookies well apart from each other as they will spread while baking.

7. Bake for 13–15 minutes until spread out and just turning golden brown. Allow to cool before removing from the baking trays.

These scrumptious macaroons are baked the Southern American way with condensed milk, making them moist and sweet. Don't overbake as they may dry out.

Coconut Macaroons

MAKES 30-35 MACAROONS

370ml (12½ fl oz) SWEETENED CONDENSED MILK
370g (12½ oz) DESICCATED COCONUT
1 tsp VANILLA EXTRACT
2 LARGE EGG WHITES

1. Preheat the oven to 160°C (320°F), Gas mark 3, and line three baking trays with baking parchment.

2. In a medium mixing bowl, mix together the condensed milk, coconut and vanilla extract. In a freestanding electric mixer with the whisk attachment or using a hand-held electric whisk, whisk the egg whites until they form stiff peaks. Carefully fold the egg whites into the coconut mixture.

3. Spoon the mixture onto the prepared baking trays — roughly 1 tablespoon per cookie. Keep them about 3–4cm (1¼–1½in) apart. Bake for 20–30 minutes or until golden brown. Allow to cool completely before serving.

Tangy and sweet, these are more cookie-like than French macaroons. Take care when removing from the baking tray as they do tend to crack.

Lemon Macaroons

MAKES 15-20 MACAROONS

3 EGG WHITES
¼ tsp CREAM OF TARTAR
½ tsp VANILLA EXTRACT
GRATED ZEST OF 1 LEMON
230g (8oz) ICING SUGAR, SIFTED
115g (4oz) GROUND ALMONDS

EQUIPMENT
PIPING BAG WITH A WIDE NOZZLE

1. Preheat the oven to 180°C (350°F), Gas mark 4, and line three baking trays with baking parchment.

2. Using a hand-held electric whisk or a freestanding electric mixer with the whisk attachment, whisk the egg whites until frothy. Add the cream of tartar and vanilla extract, then continue to whisk the egg whites until they are thick, white and glossy.

3. Using a rubber spatula, gently and gradually fold in the lemon zest, icing sugar and ground almonds.

4. Put the mixture into the piping bag and pipe cookies onto the prepared baking trays, each about 5cm (2in) in diameter as they will spread. (Alternatively, you can use a dessertspoon to spoon the mixture onto the trays in dollops, but your macaroons will come out less evenly shaped.) Make sure to keep the cookies about 5cm (2in) apart from each other on the tray.

5. Bake for approximately 10–15 minutes or until a golden colour and a nice shell has formed. Allow to cool slightly and then remove from the baking sheet using a palette knife. Be careful as they can stick and easily crack. Allow to cool completely on a wire rack before serving.

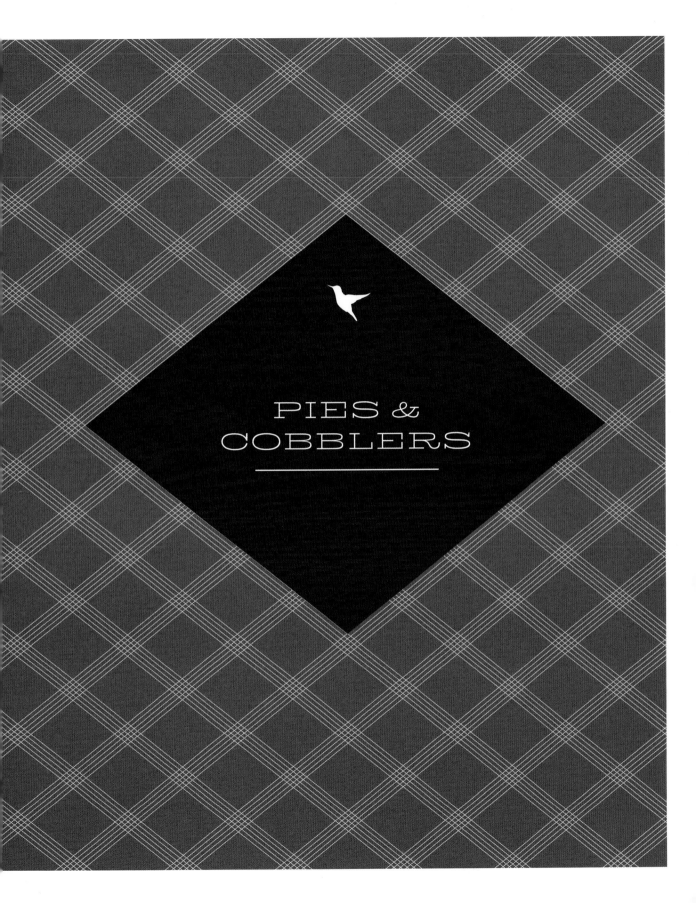

PIES & COBBLERS

This simple recipe forms the base for many of our delicious American pies. Remember to chill the dough in the fridge as instructed — it's important that the dough relaxes before it bakes.

Basic Pie Crust

MAKES 475g (1lb 1oz) (ENOUGH FOR A 23cm/9in PIE CRUST)

110g (4oz) COLD UNSALTED BUTTER, CUBED
225g (8oz) PLAIN FLOUR, PLUS EXTRA FOR DUSTING
80g (3oz) CASTER SUGAR
1 LARGE EGG

EQUIPMENT
ONE 23cm (9in) DIAMETER PIE DISH

1. Using a freestanding electric mixer with the paddle attachment or a hand-held electric mixer, mix the butter and flour together until there are no lumps of butter and a fine crumb consistency is formed. Add the caster sugar and mix through. Add the egg and mix until a dough starts to form. Don't overwork the pastry or it will become stiff and brittle.

2. Turn the pastry out onto a lightly floured surface and bring it together until smooth and even. Form into a ball and flatten slightly, then wrap the pastry in cling film and place in the fridge to rest for approximately 30–40 minutes.

3. Once the pastry has rested, roll it out on a lightly floured surface until it is about 5mm (¼in) thick. Line the pie dish with the pastry, pressing it gently into the base to make sure it is sitting neatly in the dish.

4. Trim any excess around the edges with a small knife, cutting in line with the edge of the pie dish.

5. Texture can be added to the edge of the pastry by pinching with your fingers or using a fork. Allow the pie crust to rest in the fridge again for approximately 20 minutes.

6. To bake 'blind', preheat the oven to 170°C (325°F), Gas mark 3. Line the pie crust loosely with baking parchment and fill with ceramic baking beans (or uncooked dry kidney beans). Blind-bake the pie for 10 minutes with the baking beans. Then remove the baking beans and paper and continue to bake for a further 15–20 minutes or until the crust is an even golden brown colour. Allow to cool before filling.

We love taking pies and other desserts and making them into cupcakes. However, this time we wanted to go the other way and turn the idea of our Blackbottom Cupcakes into a pie, and this is what we came up with. You can also make this recipe in individual pie cases to wow your friends.

Blackbottom Pie

SERVES 8-10

FOR THE CRUST

200g (7oz) DOUBLE CHOCOLATE COOKIES, CRUSHED INTO CRUMBS IN A FOOD PROCESSOR OR WITH A ROLLING PIN

80g (3oz) UNSALTED BUTTER, MELTED

FOR THE FILLING

3 tbsp RUM

1 tbsp WATER

2 LEAVES OF GELATINE

500ml (18fl oz) WHOLE MILK

4 EGG YOLKS

160g (5½oz) CASTER SUGAR

1 tbsp CORNFLOUR

170g (6oz) DARK CHOCOLATE (MINIMUM 70% COCOA SOLIDS), CHOPPED

FOR THE TOPPING

400ml (14fl oz) DOUBLE CREAM

3 tbsp ICING SUGAR

20g (¾oz) DARK CHOCOLATE (MINIMUM 70% COCOA SOLIDS), SHAVED WITH A PEELER

EQUIPMENT

ONE 23cm (9in) DIAMETER PIE DISH

1. Preheat the oven to 170°C (325°F), Gas mark 3.

2. To make the crust, mix together the chocolate cookie crumbs and melted butter in a medium mixing bowl. Stir together until it forms a wet sand appearance and can be squeezed together.

3. Press the crumb mixture into the base of the pie dish. Bake the base for approximately 10 minutes. Allow to cool completely.

4. Meanwhile, make the filling. In a medium mixing bowl, mix the rum and water together. Add the gelatine, and leave to soften.

5. In a medium pan, mix together the milk, egg yolks, sugar and cornflour. Whisk until all the ingredients are incorporated. Bring to the boil over a medium heat, whisking constantly. The mixture should thicken and needs to cook for about 4–5 minutes, but be careful not to overcook or the eggs may begin to scramble. Remove from the heat and add the softened gelatine leaves, water and rum. Stir through the hot mixture until the gelatine has completely dissolved.

6. Place the chopped dark chocolate in a medium bowl, and pour half of the hot mix over it. Stir until all of the chocolate has melted. Pour the chocolate filling into the prepared crust and smooth with a palette knife or the back of a spoon so that it is flat and even. Cover lightly with cling film and refrigerate for approximately 40 minutes. Cover the remaining half of the filling with cling film and set aside.

7. Once the chocolate filling has cooled, remove the pie from the fridge and carefully pour the remaining filling on top of it. Place the pie back in the fridge to set for a couple of hours or preferably overnight.

8. Once set, make the cream topping. In a medium bowl, whip up the double cream and icing sugar until it forms soft peaks. Top the chilled pie with the whipped cream and sprinkle with chocolate shavings.

We're surprised this pie lasted long enough to photograph. It's hard not to stop sneaky hands from demolishing this as soon as it comes out of the oven! Try to let it cool and set completely in the fridge. You can use other nuts instead for the brittle.

Blondie Pie

SERVES 8-10

FOR THE BRITTLE
200g (7oz) WHOLE ALMONDS (WITHOUT SKINS)

240g (8½oz) CASTER SUGAR

150ml (5½fl oz) WATER

FOR THE CRUST
250g (9oz) PLAIN FLOUR

80g (3oz) CASTER SUGAR

180g (6½oz) COLD UNSALTED BUTTER, CUBED

FOR THE FILLING
240g (8½oz) WHITE CHOCOLATE, CHOPPED

80g (3oz) UNSALTED BUTTER

3 LARGE EGG YOLKS

60g (2oz) CASTER SUGAR

150ml (5½fl oz) DOUBLE CREAM

EQUIPMENT
ONE 23cm (9in) DIAMETER PIE DISH

1. To make the brittle, line a baking tray with baking parchment and preheat the oven to 170°C (325°F), Gas mark 3. Spread the almonds in a single layer over the tray. Roast the almonds for 5-10 minutes or until light golden in colour, checking often as they will brown quickly. Set aside for later.

2. In a small pan, dissolve the sugar in the water and bring to the boil. Boil the mixture until it is a deep caramel colour. Do not stir while the caramel is boiling or it will crystallise; just gently swirl the pan from time to time. Carefully pour the hot caramel over the roasted nuts. Leave to cool completely and set.

3. In a freestanding electric mixer with the paddle attachment or using a hand-held electric mixer, mix the flour, sugar and butter together for the crust until it forms a sandy consistency. Increase the speed of the mixer, and mix until it forms a dough. Press the dough into the pie dish, making sure it is spread evenly over the base and up the sides of the dish. Place the crust in the fridge to cool and rest while you make the filling.

4. For the filling, melt the white chocolate and butter together in a microwave-safe bowl in the microwave, or alternatively in a heatproof bowl set over a pan of simmering water.

5. In the freestanding electric mixer with the whisk attachment or using a hand-held electric whisk, beat together the egg yolks and sugar until light and fluffy. Pour the melted chocolate and butter into the egg mixture, and mix well. This will split at this point, but don't worry. Pour the double cream into the mixture, whisking until the filling is smooth.

6. Break the almond brittle into rough pieces. In a food processor with the blade attachment, blitz the brittle into rough crumbs, without any large pieces. Stir half the brittle crumbs into the pie filling mixture.

7. Pour the filling into the prepared crust and bake the pie at 160°C (320°F), Gas mark 3, for approximately 30–35 minutes or until a golden colour with a very slight wobble in the middle. Leave to cool slightly before putting into the fridge to cool and set completely. Sprinkle the remaining brittle crumbs over the top of the pie before serving.

This real old-fashioned Southern dessert uses tinned peaches and can therefore be made all year round. The cobbler mix is very soft when raw, but will bake into a lovely light, spongy, scone-like topping.

Peach Cobbler

SERVES 6-8

FOR THE FILLING

3 x 400g (14oz) TINS OF SLICED PEACHES (IN JUICE)

50g (1¾oz) SOFT LIGHT BROWN SUGAR

20g (¾in) CASTER SUGAR

½ tsp MIXED SPICE

1 tsp LEMON JUICE

2 tsp CORNFLOUR

FOR THE TOPPING

170g (6oz) PLAIN FLOUR

60g (2oz) CASTER SUGAR, PLUS 3 tbsp FOR SPRINKLING

50g (1¾oz) SOFT LIGHT BROWN SUGAR

1 tsp BAKING POWDER

½ tsp SALT

120g (4oz) COLD UNSALTED BUTTER, CUBED

60ml (2fl oz) BOILING WATER

1 tsp MIXED SPICE

EQUIPMENT

ONE DEEP 23cm (9in) DIAMETER PIE DISH OR CERAMIC BAKING DISH

1. Strain the peaches of any juice. In a large mixing bowl, mix together the peach slices, sugars, mixed spice, lemon juice and cornflour. Mix well, making sure to coat the peaches in all the ingredients. Place the peach filling into the pie or baking dish.

2. Preheat the oven to 180°C (350°F), Gas mark 4. To make the topping, mix together the flour, sugars, baking powder and salt in a medium bowl. Rub the butter in with your fingertips until the mix forms a coarse breadcrumb consistency. Add the boiling water, mixing it through with a fork until just combined. This should form a soft, doughy consistency.

3. Using a spoon or fingers, drop small pieces of the dough over the top of the peaches, covering the entire dish. In a small bowl, mix together the remaining 3 tablespoons of caster sugar and the mixed spice. Sprinkle this over the top of the dough.

4. Bake the cobbler for approximately 35–40 minutes or until the topping is a rich golden brown. Allow to cool slightly before serving.

We have gone all out for this amazing pie – no holds barred. To us it epitomises the utmost in extravagant American desserts. We also love to use crushed salted pretzels over the top instead of peanuts.

Candy Bar Pie

SERVES 8-10

FOR THE CRUST

125g (4½oz) OREO BISCUITS

125g (4½oz) DIGESTIVE BISCUITS

150g (5½oz) UNSALTED BUTTER, MELTED

FOR THE FILLING

3 SNICKERS BARS

230g (8oz) FULL-FAT CREAM CHEESE
(SUCH AS PHILADELPHIA)

100g (3½oz) CASTER SUGAR

80g (3oz) SOURED CREAM

140g (5oz) CRUNCHY PEANUT BUTTER

2 LARGE EGGS

FOR THE TOPPING

140g (5oz) DARK CHOCOLATE CHIPS
(MINIMUM 70% COCOA SOLIDS)

2 tbsp DOUBLE CREAM

50g (1¾oz) SALTED PEANUTS, ROUGHLY CHOPPED

EQUIPMENT

ONE 23cm (9in) DIAMETER PIE DISH

1. Put the Oreo and digestive biscuits in a large ziplock bag or mixing bowl and crush into crumbs with a rolling pin. Place both types of cookie crumbs into a medium mixing bowl. Pour the melted butter onto the cookie crumbs. Stir using a wooden spoon, making sure the butter is evenly mixed through the crumbs.

2. Press the mixture into the pie dish, making sure to press it up the sides of the dish. Place the crust in the fridge to set for approximately an hour.

3. Preheat the oven to 160°C (320°F), Gas mark 3. Cut the Snickers bars into 5mm (¼in) pieces, and arrange them over the base of the pie crust.

4. Using a freestanding electric mixer with the paddle attachment or a hand-held electric whisk, beat the cream cheese and sugar until light and fluffy. Add the soured cream and peanut butter, mixing on a low speed until well combined.

5. Add the eggs one at a time, mixing well after each addition. Spoon the mixture into the pie crust, evenly covering all the Snickers pieces.

6. Bake the pie for approximately 35–40 minutes or until it has a light golden colour and has set with only a slight wobble in the centre. Leave the pie to cool for about an hour, and then cover it with cling film and leave to set in the fridge for a couple of hours or overnight.

7. To make the topping, place the chocolate chips and double cream in a small microwave-safe bowl in the microwave and melt the chocolate, stirring at intervals. Alternatively, melt in a small heatproof bowl set over a pan of simmering water. This should be a smooth mixture. Drizzle the chocolate over the top of the chilled pie and sprinkle with the chopped salted peanuts.

Every self-respecting American diner has a Cherry Pie on the counter for a dessert, afternoon treat or comforting late-night indulgence. Warm up slices and serve with vanilla ice-cream. It's best to use a sour cherry variety to achieve that delicious sweet-sour taste. The cherries can be fresh, frozen or tinned — just keep the weight the same.

Cherry Pie

SERVES 8-10

FOR THE CRUST

220g (8oz) COLD UNSALTED BUTTER, CUBED

450g (1lb) PLAIN FLOUR, PLUS EXTRA FOR DUSTING

160g (5½oz) CASTER SUGAR, PLUS EXTRA FOR SPRINKLING

3 LARGE EGGS

FOR THE FILLING

700g (1½lb) FRESH, TINNED OR FROZEN (THEN THAWED) PITTED CHERRIES,

150g (5½oz) CASTER SUGAR

30g (1oz) CORNFLOUR

½ tsp VANILLA EXTRACT

EQUIPMENT

ONE 23cm (9in) DIAMETER PIE DISH

1. In a freestanding electric mixer with the paddle attachment or using a hand-held electric mixer, mix the butter and flour together until there are no lumps of butter. Add the caster sugar and mix through. Add two of the eggs and mix until a dough starts to form. Don't overwork the pastry.

2. Turn the dough out onto a lightly floured surface and bring it together with your hands. Form the dough into a ball, flatten it slightly and wrap it in cling film. Place the dough in the fridge to rest for 30–40 minutes.

3. Roll the rested dough out on a lightly floured surface — it should be about 5mm (¼in) thick. Line the pie dish with the pastry, pressing it gently into the base to make sure it is sitting neatly in the dish.

4. Using a small knife, trim the edges in line with the pie dish. Gather up the offcuts to use for the lid, rewrap and put back in the fridge until needed.

5. Break the remaining egg into a small bowl and beat using a fork or small whisk. Using a pastry brush, paint a thin coating of beaten egg over the inside of the pie crust. This will create a barrier between the wet pie filling and raw pastry while they bake to prevent the bottom of the pie becoming soggy. Allow the pie crust to rest in the fridge again for approximately 20 minutes.

6. Meanwhile make the cherry filling. Drain 200ml (7fl oz) of the juice from the cherries, if using tinned, into a medium pan (make up with water if need be). Add the sugar, cornflour and vanilla extract to the cherry liquid. Mix well with a whisk to make sure there are no lumps of cornflour.

7. Place the pan over a medium heat and bring the mixture to the boil, while whisking continuously. This should boil for at least 3 minutes or until it has thickened. Add the cherries to the hot mixture, stirring to coat all the fruit. Spoon the filling into the prepared pie crust.

Recipe continues ...

8. To make the lid for the pie, roll the remaining dough out on a lightly floured surface, again to about 5mm (¼in) thick. Brush beaten egg onto the edges of the pastry in the dish, then carefully lift the pastry lid and cover the filled pie. Press down around the edges to seal. The edges can be textured with a fork or pinched with your fingers.

9. Lightly brush beaten egg over the top of the lid and sprinkle with caster sugar. Cut three small slits in the top of the pie to release steam while baking. Allow the pie to rest for another 30 minutes in the fridge.

10. Preheat the oven to 170°C (325°F), Gas mark 3.

11. Bake the pie for approximately 1 hour. Once baked, remove the pie from the oven and set aside to cool. Place in the fridge to cool and set. Allow the pie to come back to room temperature before serving.

The slight saltiness of the nuts on top of this pie works so nicely.
Make sure you take time when making the filling so as not to overcook.
And leave it to set in the fridge before tucking in!

Caramel Pie

SERVES 8–10

FOR THE CRUST

110g (4oz) COLD UNSALTED BUTTER, CUBED

225g (8oz) PLAIN FLOUR, PLUS EXTRA FOR DUSTING

80g (3oz) CASTER SUGAR

1 LARGE EGG

FOR THE FILLING

400g (14oz) CASTER SUGAR

60g (2oz) PLAIN FLOUR

500ml (18fl oz) WHOLE MILK

4 LARGE EGG YOLKS

60g (2oz) CORNFLOUR

PINCH OF SALT

100ml (3½fl oz) WATER

FOR THE TOPPING AND DECORATION

350ml (12fl oz) DOUBLE CREAM

20g (¾oz) DARK CHOCOLATE (MINIMUM 70% COCOA SOLIDS)

20g (¾oz) CHOPPED MIXED NUTS, TOASTED (SEE PAGE 119)

EQUIPMENT

ONE 23cm (9in) DIAMETER PIE DISH

1. Using a freestanding electric mixer with the paddle attachment or a hand-held electric mixer, mix the butter and flour together until there are no lumps of butter and a fine crumb consistency is formed. Add the caster sugar and mix through. Add the egg and mix until a dough starts to form. Don't overwork the pastry or it will become stiff and brittle.

2. Turn the pastry out onto a lightly floured surface and bring it together by hand until smooth and even. Form into a ball and flatten slightly, then wrap in cling film and place in the fridge to rest for approximately 30–40 minutes.

3. Once the pastry has rested, roll it out on a lightly floured surface until it is about 5mm (¼in) thick. Line the pie dish with the pastry, pressing it gently into the base to make sure it is sitting neatly in the dish.

4. Trim any excess edges with a small knife, neatly in line with the edge of the pie dish. Texture can be added to the edge of the pastry by pinching it between your fingers or using a fork. Allow the pie crust to rest in the fridge again for approximately 20 minutes.

5. To bake 'blind', preheat the oven to 170°C (325°F), Gas mark 3. Line the pie crust loosely with baking parchment and fill with ceramic baking beans (or uncooked dry kidney beans). Blind-bake the pie for 10 minutes with the baking beans. Then remove the baking beans and paper and continue to bake for a further 15–20 minutes or until the crust is an even golden brown colour. Allow to cool before filling.

6. To make the custard for the filling, mix together 200g (7oz) of the caster sugar with the flour, milk, egg yolks, cornflour and salt in a medium pan. Bring this to the boil, whisking continuously until it thickens. The custard must boil for 4–5 minutes to allow the flour to cook properly. Be careful not to overcook or the eggs may begin to scramble. Remove from the heat and immediately pour into a bowl. Set aside, covered directly with cling film to prevent a skin forming.

Recipe continues …

7. In a small pan, mix the remaining 200g (7oz) of caster sugar with the water. Over a low heat, stir gently until the sugar has dissolved. Then bring the mixture to the boil on a medium heat – don't stir while it is boiling as the sugar will crystallise. Let it boil for 15–20 minutes or until it becomes a lovely light caramel colour, then remove the pan from the heat and leave the caramel to cool for just a couple of minutes – the heat from the pan will continue to cook the caramel and it will become darker. Carefully pour the hot caramel into the prepared custard, stirring continuously while pouring. Stir thoroughly to make sure that the caramel is evenly mixed through the custard.

8. Pour the filling into the baked pie crust. Place the pie in the fridge for approximately 1 hour to set completely.

9. Using the freestanding electric mixer with the whisk attachment or a hand-held electric whisk, whip up the double cream to soft peaks. Top the pie with the whipped cream. Make chocolate shavings by using a vegetable peeler to shave away thin bits of chocolate. Sprinkle the chocolate shavings and mixed nuts over the top of the pie.

This recipe is rarely seen outside the American South even though it originated in England. The pastry case is filled with a delicious vanilla custard filling, made extra special with the addition of cornmeal. It'll crack on top; so don't expect a perfect finish. Allow the pie to cool down completely before enjoying with a cup of coffee.

Chess Pie

SERVES 8–10

FOR THE CRUST

110g (4oz) COLD UNSALTED BUTTER, CUBED

225g (8oz) PLAIN FLOUR, PLUS EXTRA FOR DUSTING

80g (3oz) CASTER SUGAR

1 LARGE EGG

FOR THE FILLING

100g (3½oz) UNSALTED BUTTER, SOFTENED

400g (14oz) CASTER SUGAR

1 tsp VANILLA EXTRACT

4 LARGE EGGS

60ml (2fl oz) DOUBLE CREAM

1 tbsp FINE CORNMEAL

1 tbsp WHITE VINEGAR

EQUIPMENT

ONE 23cm (9in) DIAMETER PIE DISH

1. Using a freestanding electric mixer with the paddle attachment or a hand-held electric mixer, mix the butter and flour together until there are no lumps of butter and a fine crumb consistency is formed. Add the caster sugar and mix through. Add the egg and mix until a dough starts to form. Don't overwork the pastry or it will become stiff and brittle.

2. Turn the pastry out onto a lightly floured surface and bring it together by hand until smooth and even. Form into a ball and flatten slightly, then wrap the pastry in cling film and place in the fridge to rest for approximately 30–40 minutes.

3. Once the pastry has rested, roll it out on a lightly floured surface until it is about 5mm (¼in) thick. Line a 23cm (9in) pie dish with the pastry, pressing it gently into the base to make sure it is sitting neatly in the dish.

4. Trim any excess around the edges with a small knife, cutting in line with the edge of the pie dish.

5. Texture can be added to the edge of the pastry by pinching with your fingers or using a fork. Allow the pie crust to rest in the fridge again for approximately 20 minutes.

6. To bake 'blind', preheat the oven to 170°C (325°F), Gas mark 3. Line the pie crust loosely with baking parchment and fill with ceramic baking beans (or uncooked dry kidney beans). Blind-bake the pie for 10 minutes with the baking beans. Then remove the baking beans and paper and continue to bake for a further 15–20 minutes or until the crust is an even golden brown colour. Allow to cool before filling.

7. To make the filling, in the freestanding electric mixer with the paddle attachment or using a hand-held electric whisk, cream together the butter, caster sugar and vanilla extract until well combined. Add the eggs one at a time, mixing well after each addition. In a separate jug, mix together the double cream, cornmeal and vinegar, whisking until smooth. Add the cream mixture to the butter and eggs. Mix well on a slow speed until all the ingredients are evenly incorporated.

8. Pour the filling into the blind-baked pie crust. Increase the oven temperature to 200°C (400°F), Gas mark 6, and bake the pie for 10 minutes, then drop the temperature to 150°C (300°F), Gas mark 2, and continue to bake for another 40–45 minutes, or until the pie seems set, with only a very slight wobble in the centre.

9. Allow the pie to cool and then refrigerate for a couple of hours or preferably overnight.

We think a cross between a dessert and a pie comes very close to pudding perfection! Please use dark chocolate with a minimum of 70 per cent cocoa solids for the filling to set properly.

Chocolate Pudding Pie

SERVES 8-10

FOR THE CRUST

200g (7oz) DOUBLE CHOCOLATE COOKIES

80g (3oz) UNSALTED BUTTER, MELTED

FOR THE FILLING

3 tbsp CORNFLOUR

1 tbsp COCOA POWDER, SIFTED

125ml (4½fl oz) DOUBLE CREAM

430ml (15fl oz) WHOLE MILK

120g (4oz) DARK CHOCOLATE (MINIMUM 70% COCOA SOLIDS), CHIPS OR CHOPPED

200g (7oz) CASTER SUGAR

40g (1½oz) UNSALTED BUTTER

1 tsp VANILLA EXTRACT

FOR THE TOPPING AND DECORATION

300ml (10½fl oz) DOUBLE CREAM

2 tbsp ICING SUGAR

20g (¾oz) DARK CHOCOLATE (MINIMUM 70% COCOA SOLIDS)

EQUIPMENT

ONE 23cm (9in) DIAMETER PIE DISH

1. Preheat the oven to 170°C (325°F), Gas mark 3.

2. In a food processor with the blade attachment, blitz the cookies into rough crumbs. In a medium mixing bowl, mix together the chocolate cookie crumbs and the melted butter. Stir until the mixture resembles wet sand and can be squeezed together.

3. Press the crumb mixture into the base of the pie dish. Bake the crust for approximately 10 minutes. Allow to cool completely.

4. In a medium bowl, mix together the cornflour and cocoa powder. Add 3–4 tablespoons of the double cream and stir to form a paste. Mix in the rest of the double cream, stirring to incorporate all the ingredients. Set this aside for later.

5. In a medium/large pan, heat up the milk, chocolate and caster sugar over a medium heat, stirring constantly until all the chocolate is completely melted. Remove the pan from the heat.

6. Whisk a small amount of the hot chocolate mixture into the cornflour and cream mixture. Whisk well to avoid lumps. Pour this back into the pan of warm chocolate milk, whisking to combine. Return the pan to the heat and bring to the boil, whisking constantly. The mixture must boil for at least 4–5 minutes to cook the cornflour.

7. Remove from the heat and stir in the butter and vanilla extract. Pour the filling into the prepared pie crust. Cover directly with cling film to prevent a skin from forming and refrigerate for at least a couple of hours until completely set and cold.

8. To top the pie, whip up the double cream and icing sugar using a freestanding electric mixer with the whisk attachment or a hand-held electric whisk, until it forms soft peaks. Spoon the cream onto the top of the pie, spreading it carefully to the edges. Texture the cream with the back of a spoon.

9. Make chocolate shavings by using a vegetable peeler to peel pieces from a slab of chocolate. Sprinkle the shavings over the top of the pie and serve.

You can use fresh peaches for this light, summery pie, but make sure they're really ripe. Serve at room temperature so that the filling has time to firm up, either on its own or with cream or custard.

Peach Pie

SERVES 8-10

FOR THE CRUST

220g (8oz) COLD UNSALTED BUTTER, CUBED

450g (1lb) PLAIN FLOUR, PLUS EXTRA FOR DUSTING

160g (5½oz) CASTER SUGAR, PLUS EXTRA FOR SPRINKLING

3 LARGE EGGS

FOR THE FILLING

700g (1½lb) DRAINED TINNED SLICED PEACHES

50g (1¾oz) CASTER SUGAR

30g (1oz) CORNFLOUR

½ tsp VANILLA EXTRACT

½ tsp GROUND CINNAMON

¼ tsp GROUND NUTMEG

EQUIPMENT

ONE 23cm (9in) DIAMETER PIE DISH

1. In a freestanding electric mixer with the paddle attachment or using a hand-held electric mixer, mix the butter and flour together until there are no lumps of butter and a fine crumb consistency is formed. Add the caster sugar and mix through. Add two of the eggs and mix until a dough starts to form. Don't overwork the pastry.

2. Turn the dough out onto a lightly floured surface and bring it together with your hands. Form the dough into a ball, press to flatten it slightly and wrap it in cling film. Place in the fridge to rest for 30–40 minutes.

3. Roll the rested dough out on a lightly floured surface — it should be about 5mm (¼in) thick. Line the pie dish with the pastry, pressing it gently into the base. Using a small knife, trim the edges in line with the pie dish. Gather up the offcuts to use for the lid, rewrap and put back in the fridge until needed.

4. Break the remaining egg into a small bowl and break up using a fork or small whisk. Using a pastry brush, paint a thin coating of beaten egg over the inside of the pie crust. This will create a barrier between the wet pie filling and raw pastry during baking to prevent the bottom of the pie becoming soggy. Allow the pie crust to rest in the fridge again for approximately 20 minutes.

5. Meanwhile, make the filling. In a medium mixing bowl, mix together the peaches, caster sugar, cornflour, vanilla and spices. Mix well to make sure that the peaches are evenly coated in the other ingredients. Spoon the filling into the prepared pie crust.

6. To make the lid for the pie, roll the remaining dough out on a lightly floured surface, again to about 5mm (¼in) thick. Brush beaten egg onto the edges of the pastry lining the dish, then carefully lift the pastry lid and cover the filled pie. Press down around the edge to seal. The edges can be textured with a fork or pinched with your fingers.

Recipe continues …

7. Lightly brush beaten egg over the top of the lid and sprinkle with caster sugar. Cut three small slits in the top of the pie to release steam while baking. Allow the pie to rest for another 30 minutes in the fridge.

8. Preheat the oven to 170°C (325°F), Gas mark 3.

9. Bake the pie for approximately 1 hour. Once baked, remove the pie from the oven and set aside to cool. Place in the fridge to cool and set, then allow the pie to come back to room temperature before serving.

* The peaches in this recipe can be fresh, frozen or tinned.

* This recipe also works well with ripe plums or nectarines.

If you've never heard of Shoofly Pie, we urge you to try it. It is simple to bake and utterly delicious. This pie was made famous by the German settlers in Pennsylvania and is based around three yummy ingredients: molasses, butter and brown sugar. We've adapted it slightly, using easy-to-find British ingredients.

Shoofly Pie

SERVES 8–10

FOR THE CRUST

110g (4oz) COLD UNSALTED BUTTER, CUBED

225g (8oz) PLAIN FLOUR, PLUS EXTRA FOR DUSTING

80g (3oz) CASTER SUGAR

1 LARGE EGG

FOR THE CRUMBS

150g (5½oz) PLAIN FLOUR

110g (4oz) SOFT DARK BROWN SUGAR

30g (1oz) COLD UNSALTED BUTTER, CUBED

PINCH OF SALT

FOR THE FILLING

¾ tsp BICARBONATE OF SODA

190ml (6½fl oz) BOILING WATER

110g (4oz) BLACK TREACLE

110g (4oz) GOLDEN SYRUP

1 LARGE EGG

1 tsp VANILLA EXTRACT

EQUIPMENT

ONE 23cm (9in) DIAMETER PIE DISH

1. First, make the pie crust. In a freestanding electric mixer with the paddle attachment or using a hand-held electric mixer, mix the butter and flour together until crumb-like in consistency. Add the caster sugar and mix through. Add the egg and mix until a dough starts to form. Don't overwork the pastry or it will become stiff and brittle.

2. Turn the dough out onto a lightly floured surface and bring it together with your hands. Form the dough into a ball, press gently to flatten and wrap it in cling film. Place the dough in the fridge to rest for 30–40 minutes.

3. Roll the rested dough out on a lightly floured surface to about 5mm (¼in) thick. Line the pie dish with the pastry, pressing it gently into the base to make sure it is sitting neatly in the dish. Using a small knife, trim the edges in line with the pie dish. Allow the pie crust to rest in the fridge again for approximately 20 minutes.

4. To bake 'blind', preheat the oven to 170°C (325°F), Gas mark 3. Line the pie crust loosely with baking parchment and fill with ceramic baking beans (or uncooked dry kidney beans). Blind-bake the pie for approximately 10 minutes with the baking beans. Then remove the baking beans and paper and continue to bake for a further 15–20 minutes or until the crust is an even golden brown colour. Allow to cool before filling.

5. For the crumbs, place the flour, brown sugar, butter and salt in a medium bowl. Rub together using your fingertips to form a sandy, crumb-like consistency. Remove 50g (1¾oz) and reserve for later use.

6. To make the filling, place the bicarbonate of soda in a medium mixing bowl and pour the boiling water over it. Add the black treacle, syrup, egg and vanilla extract. Whisk until combined. Add the larger quantity of crumbs to the filling and mix to combine. Pour the filling into the prepared pie crust. Sprinkle the remaining crumbs over the top of the filling.

7. Bake the pie for 40–45 minutes or until the filling puffs up and starts to look dry. Allow to cool completely before serving.

Cobblers are too often overlooked in Britain. We've mixed Bramley apples with Granny Smiths in order to balance out texture and sweetness. As with all cobblers, the mix is very soft when raw but bakes into a lovely light topping.

Apple & Blueberry Cobbler

SERVES 6–8

FOR THE FILLING

60g (2oz) UNSALTED BUTTER

2 BRAMLEY APPLES, PEELED, CORED AND SLICED

3 GRANNY SMITH APPLES, PEELED, CORED AND SLICED

50g (1¾oz) SOFT LIGHT BROWN SUGAR

20g (¾oz) CASTER SUGAR

½ tsp MIXED SPICE

200g (7oz) BLUEBERRIES

FOR THE TOPPING

170g (6oz) PLAIN FLOUR

60g (2oz) CASTER SUGAR

50g (1¾oz) SOFT LIGHT BROWN SUGAR, PLUS 3 tbsp FOR SPRINKLING

1 tsp BAKING POWDER

½ tsp SALT

120g (4oz) COLD UNSALTED BUTTER, CUBED

60ml (2fl oz) BOILING WATER

EQUIPMENT

ONE DEEP 23cm (9in) DIAMETER PIE DISH OR CERAMIC BAKING DISH

1. First make the filling. In a large pan, melt the butter. Add the apples, sugars and mixed spice. Stir thoroughly to make sure the apples are coated in the other ingredients. Cook the apples over a medium heat until they start to soften. The Bramley apples will soften first — this is fine as you want them to be quite soft. Once the apples are cooked, stir the blueberries through the mixture. Place the fruit in the pie or baking dish.

2. Preheat the oven to 180°C (350°F), Gas mark 4. To make the topping, mix together the flour, sugars, baking powder and salt in a medium bowl. Rub the butter in with your fingertips until the mix forms a coarse breadcrumb consistency. Add the boiling water, mixing it through with a fork until just combined. This should form a soft, doughy consistency.

3. Using a spoon or your fingers, drop small pieces of the dough over the top of the fruit, covering the entire dish. Sprinkle the remaining 3 tablespoons of light brown sugar generously over the top of the dough.

4. Bake the cobbler for approximately 35–40 minutes or until the topping is a rich golden brown. Allow to cool slightly before serving.

We love home baking with soured cream as it gives moisture and tang to so many desserts, balancing out the sweetness.

Soured Cream Pie

SERVES 8-10

FOR THE CRUST

110g (4oz) COLD UNSALTED BUTTER, CUBED

225g (8oz) PLAIN FLOUR, PLUS EXTRA FOR DUSTING

80g (3oz) CASTER SUGAR

1 LARGE EGG

FOR THE FILLING

4 LARGE EGGS

300g (10½oz) CASTER SUGAR

1 tbsp PLAIN FLOUR

1 tbsp GRATED LEMON ZEST

300g (10½oz) SOURED CREAM

½ tsp VANILLA EXTRACT

EQUIPMENT

ONE 23cm (9in) DIAMETER PIE DISH

1. Using a freestanding electric mixer with the paddle attachment or a hand-held electric mixer, mix the butter and flour together until there are no lumps of butter and they form a fine crumb consistency. Add the caster sugar and mix through. Add the egg and mix until a dough starts to form. Don't overwork the pastry or it will become stiff and brittle.

2. Turn the pastry out onto a lightly floured surface and bring it together by hand until smooth and even. Form into a ball and flatten slightly, then wrap the pastry in cling film and place in the fridge to rest for approximately 30–40 minutes.

3. Once the pastry has rested, roll it out on a lightly floured surface until it is about 5mm (¼in) thick. Line the pie dish with the pastry, pressing it gently into the base to make sure it is sitting neatly in the dish.

4. Using a small knife, trim the edges in line with the pie dish. Allow the pie crust to rest in the fridge again for approximately 20 minutes.

5. To bake 'blind', preheat the oven to 170°C (325°F), Gas mark 3. Line the pie crust loosely with baking parchment and fill with ceramic baking beans (or uncooked dry kidney beans). Blind-bake the pie for 10 minutes with the baking beans. Then remove the baking beans and paper and continue to bake for a further 15–20 minutes or until the crust is an even golden brown colour. Allow to cool before filling.

6. To make the filling, mix together the eggs and sugar in a medium bowl until combined. Add the flour, lemon zest, soured cream and vanilla extract. Mix well until the filling is smooth and all the ingredients are incorporated.

7. Pour the filling into the prepared pie crust. Turn down the oven to 160°C (320°F), Gas mark 3, and bake the pie for approximately 35–40 minutes or until the filling is set. Check the filling by gently shaking the pie dish. It should wobble very slightly but should not be watery.

8. Allow the pie to cool. Refrigerate until set and completely cool.

We adore the taste of baked pears, but you could use apples or apricots for this recipe instead. Just keep the weight of the fruits the same as the amount in the recipe.

Pear & Cranberry Tart

SERVES 8–10

FOR THE PEARS

195g (7oz) CASTER SUGAR

600ml (1 PINT) WATER

3 LARGE PEARS, PEELED, CORED AND HALVED

1 tbsp LEMON JUICE

2 tbsp WHISKY

1 tbsp VANILLA EXTRACT

60g (2oz) DRIED CRANBERRIES

FOR THE PASTRY

60g (2oz) CASTER SUGAR

250g (9oz) PLAIN FLOUR, PLUS EXTRA FOR DUSTING

¼ tsp SALT

115g (4oz) COLD UNSALTED BUTTER, CUBED,
PLUS EXTRA FOR GREASING

1 LARGE EGG

FOR THE FILLING

50g (1¾ oz) UNSALTED BUTTER, SOFTENED

120g (4oz) MARZIPAN, CUT INTO SMALL PIECES

1 LARGE EGG

1½ tbsp CORNFLOUR

1 tbsp WHISKY

Ingredients continue ...

1. First poach the pears. Put 150g (5½oz) of the caster sugar and the water in a medium pan. Stir over a low heat to dissolve the sugar. Add the pear halves and poach over a medium heat until the pears soften but are not falling apart. They should still be slightly firm in the centre. Strain the pears from the poaching liquid and reserve the poaching liquid.

2. In a medium bowl, mix together the remaining caster sugar with the lemon juice, whisky, vanilla extract and dried cranberries. Toss the warm poached pears in the mixture and leave to soak for a couple of hours, even overnight if possible.

3. Using a freestanding electric mixer with the paddle attachment or a hand-held electric mixer, make the pastry by mixing the sugar, flour, salt and butter together until they form a rough crumb consistency. Add the egg and mix until a dough starts to form. Don't overwork the pastry.

4. Turn the dough out onto a lightly floured surface and bring it together by hand. Once the dough is smooth and even, form it into a ball, flatten and wrap in cling film, then place in the fridge to rest for approximately 30–40 minutes.

5. Grease the tart tin with butter and lightly dust with flour.

6. Once the pastry has rested, roll it out on a lightly floured surface until it is about 5mm (¼in) thick. Carefully line the tart tin with the pastry, making sure to push it gently into each flute in the sides and neatly into the base. Trim any excess edges in line with the top of the tin using a small knife. Place the unbaked tart case in the fridge to rest for another 30 minutes.

Recipe continues ...

6. Whip up the double cream until it forms soft peaks. Fold the whipped cream into the cream cheese mixture. Spoon the filling into the baked pie crust and spread out evenly with the back of the spoon. Carefully cover with cling film and place in the freezer until frozen – this will take at least an hour.

7. To make the ganache topping, heat the cream in a microwave-safe bowl in the microwave or in a small saucepan over a gentle heat. Place the chocolate chips in a medium bowl and pour the warm cream over them. Stir until all the chocolate has melted and the mixture is smooth and glossy.

8. Carefully pour the ganache topping over the frozen pie, using the back of a spoon to spread it evenly over the top of the pie. Sprinkle with the extra macadamia nuts. Place the pie in the fridge for approximately 20 minutes to allow the ganache to set. Serve chilled.

FOR THE GLAZE

1 tsp WHISKY

1 tsp VANILLA EXTRACT

1 tsp CORNFLOUR

EQUIPMENT

ONE 30 x 10cm (12 x 4in) RECTANGULAR FLUTED
LOOSE-BOTTOMED TART TIN

7. To bake 'blind', preheat the oven to 170°C (325°F), Gas mark 3. Line the pastry loosely with baking parchment and fill with ceramic baking beans (or uncooked dry kidney beans). Blind-bake the tart case for 10 minutes with the baking beans. Then remove the baking beans and paper and continue to bake for a further 15–20 minutes until the crust is an even golden brown colour. Allow to cool completely before filling.

8. Next make the almond filling, cream together the butter and marzipan in the freestanding electric mixer with the paddle attachment or using the hand-held electric mixer until it is light and fluffy. Scrape down the sides of the bowl in between mixing to make sure the two incorporate fully. Add the egg and mix well. Add the cornflour and whisky and mix thoroughly.

9. Reduce the oven temperature to 160°C (320°F), Gas mark 3. Spread the filling evenly in the prepared tart case. Strain the pears and cranberries from the soaking liquid, reserving the liquid for the glaze. Slice the poached pear halves lengthways to about 1cm (½in) thick. Arrange the pears in the filling, pressing them down gently.

10. Sprinkle the cranberries over the pears, pressing them down gently so that they stick slightly into the filling.

11. Bake the tart for approximately 35–45 minutes, or until the filling has puffed up and is a golden brown colour. It might still be slightly pale in the middle, but as long as it has set, it is fine. Cover the pastry for the last 10 minutes or so of the cooking time if it starts looking too brown.

12. While the tart is baking, make the glaze. In a small pan, mix together the reserved soaking and poaching liquids, whisky, vanilla extract and cornflour. Bring this to the boil while whisking constantly. The liquid needs to reduce by about half and have thickened into a thick syrup consistency.

13. Once the tart is baked, allow it to cool for a couple of minutes and then, using a pastry brush, paint the glaze generously over the top of the pie. It's fine if it drips down the sides. Allow the glaze and tart to cool completely before removing from the tin.

With its dark chocolate ganache topping, this pie is heaven. We recommend sticking to macadamia nuts for this recipe; the flavour combination is just right!

White Chocolate & Macadamia Nut Pie

SERVES 8-10

FOR THE CRUST

110g (4oz) COLD UNSALTED BUTTER, CUBED

225g (8oz) PLAIN FLOUR, PLUS EXTRA FOR DUSTING

80g (3oz) CASTER SUGAR

1 LARGE EGG

FOR THE FILLING

200g (7oz) FULL-FAT CREAM CHEESE (SUCH AS PHILADELPHIA)

80g (3oz) CASTER SUGAR

200g (7oz) WHITE CHOCOLATE, CHOPPED

½ tsp GRATED ORANGE ZEST (ABOUT ½ AN ORANGE)

80g (3oz) MACADAMIA NUTS, ROASTED (SEE PAGE 119) AND CHOPPED

80ml (3fl oz) DOUBLE CREAM

FOR THE TOPPING AND DECORATION

125ml (4½fl oz) DOUBLE CREAM

110g (4oz) DARK CHOCOLATE CHIPS (MINIMUM 70% COCOA SOLIDS)

30g (1oz) MACADAMIA NUTS, ROASTED

EQUIPMENT

ONE 23cm (9in) DIAMETER PIE DISH

1. Using a freestanding electric mixer with the paddle attachment or a hand-held electric mixer, mix the butter and flour together until there are no lumps of butter and a fine crumb consistency is formed. Add the caster sugar and mix through. Add the egg and mix until a dough starts to form. Don't overwork the pastry or it will become stiff and brittle.

2. Turn the pastry out onto a lightly floured surface and bring it together by hand until smooth and even. Form into a ball and flatten slightly, then wrap the pastry in cling film and place in the fridge to rest for approximately 30–40 minutes.

3. Roll the rested dough out on a lightly floured surface to about 5mm (¼in) thick. Line the pie dish with the pastry. Using a small knife, trim the edges in line with the pie dish. Allow the pie crust to rest in the fridge again for approximately 20 minutes.

4. To bake 'blind', preheat the oven to 170°C (325°F), Gas mark 3. Line the pie crust loosely with baking parchment and fill with ceramic baking beans (or uncooked dry kidney beans). Blind-bake the pie for 10 minutes with the baking beans. Then remove the baking beans and paper and continue to bake for a further 15–20 minutes or until the crust is an even golden brown colour. Allow to cool before filling.

5. Using the freestanding electric mixer with the paddle attachment or a hand-held electric whisk, beat the cream cheese and sugar until they are smooth. Melt the white chocolate in a microwave-safe bowl in the microwave or in a heatproof bowl set over a pan of simmering water. Stir until smooth, then remove from the heat immediately, pour the melted white chocolate into the cream cheese mixture and mix thoroughly. Add the orange zest and chopped nuts and stir to incorporate evenly through the mix.

Recipe continues ...

6. Whip up the double cream until it forms soft peaks. Fold the whipped cream into the cream cheese mixture. Spoon the filling into the baked pie crust and spread out evenly with the back of the spoon. Carefully cover with cling film and place in the freezer until frozen — this will take at least an hour.

7. To make the ganache topping, heat the cream in a microwave-safe bowl in the microwave or in a small saucepan over a gentle heat. Place the chocolate chips in a medium bowl and pour the warm cream over them. Stir until all the chocolate has melted and the mixture is smooth and glossy.

8. Carefully pour the ganache topping over the frozen pie, using the back of a spoon to spread it evenly over the top of the pie. Sprinkle with the extra macadamia nuts. Place the pie in the fridge for approximately 20 minutes to allow the ganache to set. Serve chilled.

TRAYBAKES

This recipe has quite a few steps, so do read it carefully. The Kahlúa gives a lovely warm coffee taste to the topping, but you can omit the alcohol if desired, adding the same volume of strong coffee instead.

Chocolate Custard Squares

MAKES 12-15 SQUARES

FOR THE BASE

100g (3½oz) AMARETTI BISCUITS

60g (2oz) UNSALTED CASHEW NUTS

40g (1½oz) COCOA POWDER, SIFTED

100g (3½oz) CASTER SUGAR

150g (5½oz) UNSALTED BUTTER

80g (3oz) DESICCATED COCONUT

2 LARGE EGGS

FOR THE FILLING

200g (7oz) UNSALTED BUTTER, SOFTENED

4 tbsp CUSTARD POWDER

1 tsp VANILLA EXTRACT

500g (1lb 2oz) ICING SUGAR

4 tbsp WHOLE MILK

FOR THE TOPPING

150g (5½oz) DARK CHOCOLATE
(MINIMUM 70% COCOA SOLIDS), CHOPPED

25g (1oz) UNSALTED BUTTER

3 tbsp KAHLÚA

EQUIPMENT

ONE 20 x 30cm (8 x 12in) BAKING TRAY

1. Preheat the oven to 170°C (325°F), Gas mark 3, and line the baking tray with baking parchment.

2. In a food processor using the blade attachment, blitz the amaretti biscuits and cashew nuts until reduced to crumbs. Add the cocoa powder and caster sugar and blitz again until all incorporated.

3. Pour the crumbs out into a large mixing bowl. Melt the butter in a microwave-safe bowl in the microwave or in a small pan on the stove, then add the coconut and melted butter to the crumbs. Mix well to combine. Add the eggs and mix to incorporate.

4. Press the base into the prepared tin and bake for 15 minutes or until firm. Allow to cool completely before adding the topping.

5. In a freestanding electric mixer with the paddle attachment or using a hand-held electric whisk, cream the butter for the filling until light and fluffy. Add the custard powder and vanilla extract, then add the icing sugar and mix until the mixture becomes crumbly. Add the milk and mix well until the filling is smooth and light.

6. Spoon the custard filling over the cooled base and smooth out evenly. Place in the fridge to chill and set completely for about 1 hour.

7. Next make the chocolate topping. In a glass bowl over a pan of simmering water or in a microwave-safe bowl in the microwave, melt the chocolate and butter together. Once melted, add the Kahlúa and mix until it is smooth and glossy. This might split initially, but continue to mix and it will come back together.

8. Spoon the topping over the set custard, smoothing it evenly over the top. Place in the fridge to set completely for several hours.

9. Once set, take the bar out of the tin and place on a chopping board. Peel away the baking parchment from the sides and portion the bar into 12–15 pieces (or as many as desired).

Sticky, blueberry-filled loaf – this is best eaten on the day you've baked it, and it's so good that you won't want to keep it long anyway! The dough can be made into buns instead of a loaf. Simply follow steps 5, 6 and 8 in Cinnamon Buns (see pages 214–17).

Blueberry Loaf

SERVES 8-10

FOR THE DOUGH

300ml (10½fl oz) LUKEWARM WHOLE MILK

25g (1oz) CASTER SUGAR

1½ tsp DRIED ACTIVE YEAST

500g (1lb 2oz) STRONG WHITE BREAD FLOUR, PLUS EXTRA FOR DUSTING

1 tsp SALT

85g (3oz) UNSALTED BUTTER, CUBED

FOR THE FILLING

60g (2oz) UNSALTED BUTTER, SOFTENED

100g (3½oz) SOFT LIGHT BROWN SUGAR

200g (7oz) BLUEBERRIES

1 LARGE EGG, BEATEN

EQUIPMENT

ONE 900g (2lb) LOAF TIN

1. Grease the loaf tin with butter and dust with flour.

2. In a jug, mix together the lukewarm milk, caster sugar and yeast. Stir well and then set aside until it becomes frothy – this will take approximately 20 minutes.

3. In a large bowl, sift together the flour and salt. Add the butter and rub it into the dry ingredients to form a crumb-like consistency with no large lumps of butter. Make a well in the centre of the dry ingredients and pour in the milk and yeast. Using a spoon, bring the mixture together to form a dough.

4. Turn the dough out onto a lightly floured surface, and knead well until soft and smooth. Place the dough back into a large, lightly floured mixing bowl. Cover the bowl with cling film and leave in a warm place to allow the dough to rise for approximately 45 minutes or until doubled in size.

5. Once the dough has proved, remove it from the bowl and gently knock it back. Knead it gently to get the dough smooth and then roll the dough out on a lightly floured surface until it is 30 x 38cm (12 x 15in). Using a sharp knife, cut the dough lengthways into four equal strips.

6. Gently spread the soft butter evenly over the strips of dough. Sprinkle 50g (1¾oz) of the light brown sugar evenly over the dough, then sprinkle over the blueberries, gently pressing them down into the dough. Carefully lift the strips and pile them neatly on top of each other, and then cut the pile of strips into six equal square stacks. Carefully lift each stack and place it into the tin, cut side facing up. Place each stack next to one another to fill the length of the tin. Any stray blueberries can be squeezed in among the dough at this stage.

7. Wrap the tin in cling film and set aside for the dough to rise again. This will take approximately 30–40 minutes or until the dough has doubled in size.

8. Preheat the oven to 170°C (325°F), Gas mark 3. Gently brush the top of the risen loaf with beaten egg and sprinkle over the remaining light brown sugar. Bake for approximately 30–35 minutes or until golden brown. Allow to cool slightly and serve warm.

Make sure you press these bars quite firmly into the prepared tin and allow them to set completely before cutting them into slices. The mix is also great stirred into some yoghurt for breakfast.

Peanut Butter Granola Bars

MAKES 12–15 BARS

60g (2oz) UNSALTED BUTTER

60ml (2fl oz) HONEY

480g (1lb 1oz) PORRIDGE OATS

80g (3oz) FLAKED ALMONDS

80g (3oz) PECAN NUTS, CHOPPED

50g (1¾oz) PUMPKIN SEEDS

50g (1¾oz) SUNFLOWER SEEDS

½ tsp GROUND CINNAMON

160g (5½oz) RAISINS

100g (3½oz) CRUNCHY PEANUT BUTTER

125ml (4½fl oz) GOLDEN SYRUP

70g (2½oz) SOFT LIGHT BROWN SUGAR

EQUIPMENT

ONE 32 x 23cm (13 x 9in) BAKING TRAY AND TWO LARGE BAKING TRAYS

1. Preheat the oven to 170°C (325°F), Gas mark 3, and line the baking tray with baking parchment.

2. In a small pan, melt the butter and honey together.

3. In a large mixing bowl, mix together the oats, almonds, pecan nuts, pumpkin seeds and sunflower seeds, ground cinnamon and raisins. Pour the melted butter and honey over the dry ingredients and stir until combined. This will still be a dry mixture.

4. Spread the granola mixture out on the two large baking trays in a thin even layer. Bake for 20 minutes, stirring every now and then to prevent it from burning or sticking to the trays. Once the granola is golden brown in colour, remove it from the oven and allow to cool completely.

5. In a medium pan, melt the peanut butter, golden syrup and light brown sugar together. Transfer the cooled granola mix into a large mixing bowl. Pour the melted peanut butter mixture over the granola. Mix well until the granola is fully coated.

6. Press the granola into the prepared lined tray and put aside to cool completely and set. Once set, turn the bar out onto a chopping board and cut into slices.

As with all our swirly bun recipes, these are best eaten fresh and warm as they don't keep well. If you want to be extra indulgent, you could spread some chocolate hazelnut paste onto each bun before serving!

Chocolate Hazelnut Buns

MAKES 16-18 BUNS

FOR THE DOUGH

300ml (10½fl oz) LUKEWARM WHOLE MILK

25g (1oz) CASTER SUGAR

1½ tsp DRIED ACTIVE YEAST

500g (1lb 2oz) STRONG WHITE BREAD FLOUR, PLUS EXTRA FOR DUSTING

1 tsp SALT

85g (3oz) UNSALTED BUTTER, CUBED

FOR THE FILLING

50g (1¾oz) UNSALTED BUTTER, SOFTENED

100g (3½oz) CASTER SUGAR

100g (3½oz) HAZELNUTS, FINELY CHOPPED, PLUS EXTRA FOR SPRINKLING

25g (1oz) COCOA POWDER, SIFTED, PLUS EXTRA FOR SPRINKLING

1 LARGE EGG, BEATEN

FOR THE GLAZE

50g (1¾oz) UNSALTED BUTTER, SOFTENED

300g (10½oz) ICING SUGAR, SIFTED

125g (4½oz) FULL-FAT CREAM CHEESE (SUCH AS PHILADELPHIA)

EQUIPMENT

ONE 25cm (10in) DIAMETER ROUND CAKE TIN OR TWO 20cm (8in) DIAMETER TINS

1. In a jug, mix together the lukewarm milk, caster sugar and yeast. Stir well and then set aside until it becomes frothy — this takes approximately 20 minutes.

2. In a large bowl, sift together the flour and salt. Add the butter and rub it into the dry ingredients to form a crumb-like consistency with no large lumps of butter. Make a well in the centre of the dry ingredients and pour in the milk and yeast. Using a spoon, bring the mixture together to form a dough.

3. Turn the dough out onto a lightly floured surface and knead well until soft and smooth. Place the dough back into a lightly floured large mixing bowl. Cover the bowl with cling film and leave in a warm place to allow the dough to rise for approximately 40 minutes, or until doubled in size.

4. Once the dough has risen, knock it back in the bowl and turn it out onto a lightly floured surface. Knead it gently to get the dough smooth. Roll the dough out into a rough rectangle, about 1.5cm (⅔in) thick.

5. Gently spread the soft butter evenly over the dough. In a small bowl, mix the caster sugar, chopped hazelnuts and cocoa powder together. Evenly spread the hazelnut mixture over the butter on the dough and press down with the rolling pin to get the nuts to stick. Roll the dough up lengthways like a Swiss roll. Using a sharp knife, cut the roll into 16–18 slices.

6. Line the cake tin with baking parchment. Very gently place the slices, flattest side down, snugly into the tin. Wrap the tin in cling film and allow the dough to rise again for approximately 20 minutes.

Recipe continues ...

7. While the dough is rising, the glaze can be made. Put the butter in a freestanding electric mixer with a paddle attachment or use a hand-held electric whisk to gradually beat in the icing sugar until there are no lumps of butter. Add a little of the cream cheese to loosen the mixture and beat until smooth, then add the rest of the cream cheese and mix on a slow speed until incorporated. Turn the speed to high and beat the topping until it is light and fluffy. Set aside to use later.

8. Preheat the oven to 180°C (350°F), Gas mark 4. Gently brush the tops of the risen dough buns with beaten egg. Bake the buns for approximately 10–15 minutes or until golden brown. Allow to cool slightly and then top with the cream cheese glaze. Allow this to melt on top of the buns and then sprinkle over some chopped hazelnuts and dust with cocoa powder.

* See the step-by-step photographs on page 215 for preparing buns baked as in this recipe.

* The cream cheese topping can be left out.

You can substitute your favourite chocolate bars for the Mars and Snickers used in our recipe. Just make sure you keep the total weight of the chocolate bars the same. Be generous with the melted butter when you brush it onto the parcels before baking as it will help stop the pastry cracking and give a lovely crisp golden colour.

Fruit & Nut Chocolate Parcels

MAKES 12 PARCELS

50g (1¾oz) MIXED NUTS

50g (1¾oz) MIXED DRIED FRUIT

2 x 58g (2oz) SNICKERS BARS

1 x 58g (2oz) MARS BAR

1 x 270g (9½oz) PACKET OF FILO PASTRY (6 SHEETS)

75g (2½oz) UNSALTED BUTTER

ICING SUGAR, FOR DUSTING

1. Preheat the oven to 180°C (350°F), Gas mark 4, and line one or two baking trays with baking parchment.

2. Roughly chop the mixed nuts and dried fruit. Chop the chocolate bars into fine slices or small pieces.

3. On a clean chopping board, carefully unroll the filo pastry. Keep the pastry covered with a clean damp tea towel to prevent it from drying out. Melt the butter in a microwave-safe bowl in the microwave or in a small pan on the stove.

4. Peel away one sheet of the pastry and place it on a second chopping board or flat surface. Using a pastry brush, paint it with a layer of melted butter. Place a second sheet of pastry on top of the first sheet. Gently smooth it down. Brush a layer of melted butter over the second sheet.

5. Using a sharp knife, cut the pastry in half lengthways and then in half widthways to give four pieces. In each piece, place a small amount of the chopped chocolate, nuts and fruit at the bottom of one short end of the pastry.

6. Fold the two long sides inwards, partially covering the filling. Then roll up the parcel from the side closest to you, like a spring roll. When you reach the end, lightly brush the sealing end of the pastry with some melted butter, then roll to seal the parcel.

7. Repeat steps 4–6 twice to complete all the parcels.

8. Place the parcels onto the prepared baking trays, spacing them evenly apart. The seam side of each parcel needs to be on the underside. Brush the tops of all the parcels with melted butter to give them a golden crispy finish.

9. Bake for approximately 18–20 minutes or until the pastry is an even golden colour and is nice and crispy. Allow to cool for 5 minutes, then dust with a sprinkling of icing sugar and serve warm.

The much-loved American campsite treat — this time used for topping brownies! It's essential to line the baking tin with foil as this will stop any burning when it comes to putting the tin back under the grill or using a cook's blowtorch for the marshmallow topping.

S'more Brownies

MAKES 12-15 BROWNIES

FOR THE BASE
200g (7oz) DIGESTIVE BISCUITS
125g (4½oz) UNSALTED BUTTER

FOR THE BROWNIE
115g (4oz) UNSALTED BUTTER
120g (4oz) DARK CHOCOLATE
(MINIMUM 70% COCOA SOLIDS), CHOPPED
190g (7oz) SOFT LIGHT BROWN SUGAR
130g (4½oz) CASTER SUGAR
1½ tsp VANILLA EXTRACT
½ tsp SALT
4 LARGE EGGS
140g (5oz) PLAIN FLOUR, SIFTED

FOR THE TOPPING
400g (14oz) LARGE WHITE MARSHMALLOWS

EQUIPMENT
ONE 20 x 30cm (8 x 12in) BAKING TRAY
COOK'S BLOWTORCH (OPTIONAL)

1. Line the baking tray with foil, taking it right up the sides of the tray with excess at the top. Preheat the oven to 160°C (320°F), Gas mark 3.

2. To make the biscuit base, seal the biscuits in a large ziplock bag or place in a mixing bowl and crush into crumbs with a rolling pin. Place the biscuit crumbs in a medium bowl. Melt the butter in a microwave-safe bowl in the microwave or in a small pan on the stove, then pour into the crumbs and stir through, making sure all the crumbs are coated. Set aside.

3. To make the brownie, place the butter and dark chocolate in a microwave-safe bowl and melt together in the microwave, pausing to stir occasionally, until completely melted and smooth. Alternatively, place in a heatproof bowl over a pan of simmering water and stir until melted.

4. Transfer the melted chocolate into a medium mixing bowl. Add the sugars, vanilla extract and salt and stir thoroughly to make sure all the ingredients are incorporated. Add the eggs and beat vigorously to make a smooth, shiny batter. Add the flour and stir just until incorporated.

5. Pour the batter into the prepared baking tray. Sprinkle the biscuit crumb mixture evenly over the top of the uncooked brownie.

6. Bake the brownie for 30–35 minutes or until a skewer inserted in the middle comes out mostly clean.

7. Place the marshmallows in rows on top of the baked brownie and place back in the oven for 2–3 minutes to melt and soften the marshmallow. Make sure the excess foil is sticking up to prevent the marshmallow dripping over the sides of the tray.

8. Then, using a cook's blowtorch or under a grill, carefully toast the marshmallows to get a lovely golden-brown toasted colour and a crisp texture. Be careful not to let them catch alight. Allow to cool before cutting into portions with a heated knife.

Using pumpkin in desserts may seem so American, but it's definitely worth trying as it gives a sponge incredible moistness and depth of flavour. You can leave out the desiccated coconut if you like, or even dust with cocoa powder instead.

Pumpkin Bars

MAKES 18 BARS

FOR THE SPONGE

4 LARGE EGGS

250ml (9fl oz) SUNFLOWER OIL

360g (12½oz) SOFT LIGHT BROWN SUGAR

1 x 425g (15oz) TIN OF PUMPKIN PURÉE

340g (12oz) PLAIN FLOUR

2 tsp BAKING POWDER

1 tsp BICARBONATE OF SODA

1 tsp GROUND CINNAMON

1 tsp MIXED SPICE

1 tsp SALT

FOR THE TOPPING AND DECORATION

120g (4oz) FULL-FAT CREAM CHEESE (SUCH AS PHILADELPHIA)

50g (1¾oz) UNSALTED BUTTER, WELL SOFTENED

200g (7oz) ICING SUGAR

30g (1oz) DESICCATED COCONUT, TOASTED

EQUIPMENT

ONE 28 x 23cm (11 x 9in) BAKING TRAY

1. Preheat the oven to 170°C (325°F), Gas mark 3, and line the baking tray with baking parchment.

2. In a freestanding electric mixer with the paddle attachment or using a hand-held electric whisk, mix together the eggs, oil, sugar and pumpkin purée until well combined. In a separate bowl, sift together the flour, baking powder, bicarbonate of soda, spices and salt.

3. Add the dry ingredients to the pumpkin mixture and mix well until combined and it has formed a smooth, even batter.

4. Pour the batter into the prepared baking tray and bake for approximately 30 minutes or until the sponge springs back when lightly touched. Set aside and allow the sponge to cool completely before frosting.

5. While the sponge is cooling, make the topping. In the freestanding electric mixer with the paddle attachment or using the hand-held electric whisk, cream together the cream cheese and butter until well combined. Add the icing sugar and mix until incorporated. Increase the mixer or whisk speed and beat the topping until light and fluffy.

6. Carefully turn the sponge out onto a chopping board. Spoon the topping onto the sponge and spread it out evenly with a palette knife. It can be textured with the tip of the palette knife if desired. Sprinkle the toasted coconut evenly over the top.

7. Using a large knife, portion the sponge into 3 on the short side and 6 on the long edge to give 18 portions. This is only a suggestion as the bar can be cut into larger or smaller portions depending on what you require.

These cinnamon buns or rolls are also known as sticky buns in the South and it's not hard to see why when you've melted over the cream cheese glaze! Just make sure you eat them when fresh and warm and remember the cream cheese topping can be left out if you'd prefer them plain.

Cinnamon Buns

MAKES 16–18 BUNS

FOR THE DOUGH
300ml (10½ fl oz) LUKEWARM WHOLE MILK

25g (1oz) CASTER SUGAR

1½ tsp DRIED ACTIVE YEAST

500g (1lb 2oz) STRONG WHITE BREAD FLOUR, PLUS EXTRA FOR DUSTING

1 tsp SALT

85g (3oz) UNSALTED BUTTER, CUBED

FOR THE FILLING
80g (3oz) UNSALTED BUTTER, SOFTENED

80g (3oz) SOFT DARK BROWN SUGAR

1½ tsp GROUND CINNAMON

1 LARGE EGG, BEATEN

FOR THE GLAZE
50g (1¾ oz) UNSALTED BUTTER, SOFTENED

300g (10½ oz) ICING SUGAR, SIFTED

125g (4½ oz) FULL-FAT CREAM CHEESE (SUCH AS PHILADELPHIA)

EQUIPMENT
ONE 25cm (10in) DIAMETER ROUND CAKE TIN OR TWO 20cm (8in) DIAMETER TINS

1. In a jug, mix together the lukewarm milk, caster sugar and yeast. Stir well and then set aside until it becomes frothy — this takes approximately 20 minutes.

2. In a large bowl, sift together the flour and salt. Add the butter and rub it into the dry ingredients to form a crumb-like consistency with no large lumps of butter. Make a well in the centre of the dry ingredients and pour in the milk and yeast. Using a spoon, bring the mixture together to form a dough.

3. Turn the dough out onto a lightly floured surface and knead well until soft and smooth. Place the dough back into a large, lightly floured mixing bowl. Cover the bowl with cling film and leave in a warm place to allow the dough to rise for approximately 40 minutes or until doubled in size.

4. Once the dough has risen, knock it back in the bowl and turn it out onto a lightly floured surface. Knead it gently to get the dough smooth, then roll out into a rough rectangle, about 1.5cm (⅔in) thick.

5. Gently spread the soft butter evenly over the dough. In a small bowl, mix the dark brown sugar and ground cinnamon together. Sprinkle the cinnamon sugar evenly over the dough. Roll the dough up lengthways like a Swiss roll. Using a sharp knife, cut the roll into 16–18 slices.

6. Line the cake tin with baking parchment. Very gently place the slices, flattest side down, into the tin, arranging them snugly. Wrap the tin in cling film and allow the dough to rise again for approximately 20 minutes.

Recipe continues …

7. While the dough is rising, the glaze can be made. Put the butter in a freestanding electric mixer with a paddle attachment or use a hand-held electric whisk to gradually beat in the icing sugar until there are no lumps of butter. Add a little of the cream cheese to loosen the mixture and beat until smooth, then add the rest of the cream cheese and mix on a slow speed until incorporated. Turn the speed to high and beat the topping until it is light and fluffy. Set aside to use later.

8. Preheat the oven to 180°C (350°F), Gas mark 4. Gently brush the tops of the risen dough buns with beaten egg. Bake for approximately 10–15 minutes, or until golden brown. Allow to cool slightly and then top with the cream cheese glaze. Allow this to melt on top of the cinnamon buns.

SWEET TREATS & CLASSIC PUDS

Jelly rolls are the American name for Swiss rolls, with the 'jelly' referring to the sweet jam filling inside. They're best eaten on the day of baking — and you can substitute with another flavour of jam if you prefer.

Raspberry Jelly Roll

SERVES 8–10

4 EGGS, SEPARATED

180g (6½oz) CASTER SUGAR

1 tbsp VANILLA EXTRACT

120g (4oz) PLAIN FLOUR

¾ tsp BAKING POWDER

¼ tsp SALT

ICING SUGAR, FOR DUSTING

160g (5½oz) RASPBERRY JAM

EQUIPMENT

ONE 32 x 23 x 2cm (13 x 9 x ¾in) SWISS ROLL TIN

1. Preheat the oven to 180°C (350°F), Gas mark 4, and line the Swiss roll tin with baking parchment.

2. In a freestanding electric mixer with the whisk attachment or using a hand-held electric whisk, whisk the egg whites until stiff but not dry or overbeaten. Set aside.

3. Using the mixer or whisk again, in another bowl mix the egg yolks on high speed until pale. Gradually add the caster sugar and vanilla extract while still mixing on a high speed. Mix until pale and fluffy.

4. Sift together the flour, baking powder and salt. Add the sifted dry ingredients to the egg yolks and fold in until combined. Gently fold the egg whites into the batter.

5. Pour the batter into the prepared tin, making sure it is an even thickness all over the tray. Bake for 10–15 minutes or until the sponge is a light golden-brown colour.

6. Dust a clean tea towel with icing sugar. Loosen the edges of the cake and invert the sponge onto the towel.

7. Beginning at the narrow edge of the sponge, roll the sponge and the towel up together. Cool on a rack, seam side down, for 10–15 minutes.

8. Once cooled, gently unroll, peel away the paper and spread the raspberry jam over the inside of the sponge roll. Re-roll the sponge without the tea towel and dust with icing sugar just before serving.

* See page 110 for step-by-step photographs showing how best to roll up a roulade. You can use either baking parchment or a clean tea towel.

* If you are concerned about the sponge cracking as you roll it up, dampen the tea towel (if using) before turning the cake out onto it.

These traditional fairground and carnival cakes are a delicious cross between a doughnut and a cake. They're sometimes called 'funny cakes' in America for their unique appearance. These cakes never look perfect but that's the point! They are delicious on their own, sprinkled with icing sugar or cinnamon or served with jam, chocolate spread or fresh fruit.

Funnel Cakes

MAKES 8-12 CAKES

120g (4oz) UNSALTED BUTTER

1 tbsp CASTER SUGAR

250ml (9fl oz) WATER

PINCH OF SALT

170g (6oz) PLAIN FLOUR

4 LARGE EGGS

2 LARGE EGG WHITES

APPROX. 300ml (10½fl oz) SUNFLOWER OIL, FOR FRYING

ICING SUGAR, FOR DUSTING

EQUIPMENT

COOKING THERMOMETER (OPTIONAL)

PIPING BAG WITH A MEDIUM NOZZLE 8mm (⅓in) WIDE

1. In a medium pan, melt the butter with the sugar and water and bring to the boil. Once boiled, turn off the heat and add the salt and flour to the pan, stirring with a wooden spoon until a dough forms.

2. Transfer the dough to a freestanding electric mixer with the paddle attachment or use a bowl and a hand-held electric whisk. Mix for a short time, allowing the dough to cool down slightly.

3. Add the eggs and egg whites one at a time, mixing thoroughly after each addition and making sure the egg is completely incorporated before adding the next.

4. Line a baking tray with kitchen paper. In a large high-sided pan, heat up the sunflower oil to approximately 160°C (320°F). Put the batter into the piping bag. Test with a thermometer, or do the bread cube test (see page 19).

5. When the oil is hot, carefully pipe the batter straight into the pan in squiggly overlapping lines, to create a round, latticed cake. Allow this to fry for approximately 2–3 minutes on either side or until an even golden brown.

6. Carefully remove the funnel cake from the oil with a slotted spoon and place it on the prepared kitchen paper to drain the excess oil. Repeat with the remaining batter. Once all the cakes are made, dust generously with icing sugar and eat warm. These can be served with whipped cream, berries, jam, chocolate sauce — whatever your vice may be ...

✱ Piping batter into a pan takes a little practice but it's easy once you get the hang of it. Make sure you use fresh oil at the correct temperature for the best results.

You can use either salted or natural peanuts, but we prefer salted as the flavour offsets the sweetness of the brittle so well. Break up into big pieces and package up beautifully for a classic American Christmas gift.

Peanut Brittle

MAKES ABOUT 600g (1lb 5oz) BRITTLE

250g (9oz) PEANUTS, LIGHTLY SALTED OR UNSALTED
300g (10½oz) CASTER SUGAR
400ml (14fl oz) WATER

1. Line a baking tray with baking parchment and preheat the oven to 170°C (325°F), Gas mark 3.

2. If the peanuts have not been roasted, spread them out on the tray and toast them for 5–10 minutes until they are a light golden colour. Set aside to cool.

3. Put the caster sugar and water in a medium saucepan and stir over a low heat to dissolve the sugar. Then turn up the heat, bring the mixture to the boil and boil for 15–20 minutes or until it turns a rich caramel colour. Do not stir the mixture while it's boiling or the caramel will crystallise; just gently swirl the pan from time to time.

4. Carefully pour the hot caramel over the nuts, making sure to try and cover them evenly in sugar. Set aside (carefully as the tray will be hot) and leave the brittle to cool and set completely. Once cooled, break into pieces and serve.

You can drizzle these with maple syrup once cooked, but make sure you don't get them too soggy! Changing the type of nuts will vary the taste so it's worth experimenting, but try pecans if you want to give these twists that classic American flavour.

Cinnamon Pecan Twists

MAKES 20 STICKS

500g (1lb 2oz) READY-MADE PUFF PASTRY
PLAIN FLOUR, FOR DUSTING
40g (1½oz) PECAN NUTS, FINELY CHOPPED
50g (1¾oz) SOFT LIGHT BROWN SUGAR
½ tsp GROUND CINNAMON
1 LARGE EGG

1. Line two baking trays with baking parchment.

2. Roll out the puff pastry on a lightly floured surface to about 5mm (¼in) thick. Trim the edges to make a nice neat rectangle.

3. In a small bowl, mix the chopped pecan nuts, light brown sugar and ground cinnamon together. In another small bowl, lightly beat the egg to break it up.

4. Using a pastry brush, brush the egg evenly over the puff pastry rectangle. Sprinkle the nut and sugar mixture evenly over the pastry. Press it down so that it sticks.

5. Cut the rectangle widthways into 1cm (½in) thick strips. Carefully twist each strip to give a spiral appearance. Place the twists on the prepared baking trays, and then freeze for 10–15 minutes.

6. Preheat the oven to 180°C (350°F), Gas mark 4, and bake the twists for 15–20 minutes or until a golden brown colour and cooked through. These can be served warm or cool.

Yes, you really can make your own doughnuts at home! Using fresh oil, at the correct temperature, is important to get good results. These are best eaten fresh from the pan, still warm and sprinkled with plain or cinnamon sugar.

Doughnuts

MAKES 10-12 DOUGHNUTS

1 tbsp DRIED ACTIVE YEAST

60ml (2fl oz) LUKEWARM WATER

2 tbsp CASTER SUGAR, FOR THE YEAST

190ml (7fl oz) WARM WHOLE MILK

1 LARGE EGG

30g (1oz) UNSALTED BUTTER, MELTED

340g (12oz) STRONG WHITE BREAD FLOUR, PLUS EXTRA FOR DUSTING

700ml (1 pint 4fl oz) SUNFLOWER OIL, FOR FRYING

100g (3½ oz) CASTER SUGAR

2 tsp GROUND CINNAMON

EQUIPMENT

TWO ROUND COOKIE CUTTERS, ONE SMALLER THAN THE OTHER

COOKING THERMOMETER (OPTIONAL)

1. In a medium jug, dissolve the yeast in the lukewarm water with 1 tablespoon of the caster sugar. Stir to dissolve the yeast and then leave the mixture to sit for about 20 minutes or until it gets a light foam on the surface.

2. Add the milk, egg, butter and remaining sugar to the yeast mixture.

3. Place the flour in a large mixing bowl, and make a well in the centre. Pour the liquids into the well and mix the dough with your hands. Once the dough has come together, turn it out onto a lightly floured surface and knead well. The dough should be kneaded for approximately 15 minutes or until it is smooth and even.

4. Place the dough into a large mixing bowl, and cover with cling film. Put the bowl somewhere warm and leave the dough to prove for approximately 40 minutes. The dough should double in size.

5. Once the dough has proved, knock it back and roll it out on a lightly floured surface until it is about 2.5cm (1in) thick. Using the larger cookie cutter, cut out the doughnuts. Cut out the centre of the doughnuts using the smaller cutter.

6. Prepare a baking tray by lining it with kitchen paper. In a large pan, heat up the sunflower oil to approximately 170°C (325°F). Test with a thermometer or do the bread cube test (see page 19).

7. When the oil is ready, carefully lower the doughnuts into the oil using a slotted spoon. Fry the doughnuts for 4–6 minutes or until they are a golden brown colour and are floating. Turn the doughnuts in the oil to get an even colour all over. Try frying one doughnut first to check the oil temperature and cooking time as these can differ. Cut this one open to check the inside is cooked through.

8. Carefully remove the doughnuts from the oil using a slotted spoon and place them on the prepared kitchen towel to drain off any excess oil.

9. In a medium bowl, mix together the caster sugar and ground cinnamon. Toss the warm doughnuts in the cinnamon sugar to coat evenly. Serve warm.

Whenever making recipes that caramelise sugar, be sure to use a sugar thermometer for consistent results. This fudge is perfect for home-made gifts and you could even mix it up with the Vanilla Fudge on page 237.

Chocolate Fudge

MAKES 16–20 PIECES OF FUDGE

400g (14oz) CASTER SUGAR

60g (2oz) DARK CHOCOLATE
(MINIMUM 70% COCOA SOLIDS), BROKEN INTO PIECES

2 tbsp GOLDEN SYRUP

120ml (4fl oz) DOUBLE CREAM

30g (1oz) UNSALTED BUTTER

1 tsp VANILLA EXTRACT

EQUIPMENT

ONE 17.5cm (7in) SQUARE TIN

SUGAR THERMOMETER

1. Line the tin with baking parchment.

2. In a medium saucepan, heat up the sugar, chocolate, syrup and cream together. Once combined, boil without stirring until the mixture reaches the soft ball stage (see page 92) — 115°C (239°F) on a sugar thermometer.

3. Drop in the butter and leave it to melt without stirring. Leave the hot mixture to cool until it drops to 45°C (113°F). Still do not stir or disturb during this time or the fudge may become grainy.

4. Add the vanilla extract and stir the fudge vigorously until it is thick and the shine has gone. Pour the fudge into the prepared tin and leave to set for a couple of hours or preferably overnight. Don't put it in the fridge.

5. Once set, carefully turn the fudge out onto a chopping board and portion out into your desired-size pieces.

Another treat that is usually shop-bought, but tastes even better when made at home. You can use dark corn syrup, if available, rather than the golden syrup for a more American flavour — but whichever you use, a sugar thermometer is useful here.

Coconut Marshmallows

MAKES 35–40 MARSHMALLOWS

250g (9oz) DESICCATED COCONUT

SUNFLOWER OIL, FOR GREASING

3 tbsp (30g/1oz) POWDERED GELATINE

300g (10½oz) CASTER SUGAR

125g (4½oz) GOLDEN SYRUP

2 LARGE EGG WHITES

PINCH OF SALT

2 tsp VANILLA EXTRACT

EQUIPMENT

ONE 32 x 23cm (13 x 9in) BAKING TRAY

SUGAR THERMOMETER

1. Lightly toast the desiccated coconut until it is a light golden brown — this takes about 5–6 minutes in a hot oven, but keep checking as it will turn brown quite suddenly.

2. Oil the baking tray, and sprinkle with half of the toasted coconut. In a small bowl, soften the gelatine in 155ml (5½fl oz) water.

3. In a medium saucepan, heat the caster sugar, golden syrup and 125ml (4½fl oz) water, stirring until the sugar has dissolved. Bring the sugar liquid to the boil and boil until it reaches the soft ball stage — 115°C (239°F) on a sugar thermometer. Don't stir while the mixture is boiling.

4. While the mixture is boiling, start to whisk up the egg whites using a freestanding electric mixer with the whisk attachment or a hand-held electric whisk until they form soft peaks.

5. Remove the syrup from the heat when it reaches the correct temperature and leave it to cool for 3–4 minutes. Then pour the gelatine into the hot syrup, stirring gently to dissolve the gelatine. The mixture will bubble up slightly.

6. With the mixer or whisk on a slow speed, pour the hot syrup onto the egg whites. Add the salt and vanilla extract once all the syrup has been poured in — this can be done while the machine is on. Once all the syrup has been added, turn up the mixer speed to high and beat until the marshmallow has doubled in size and is thick — this can take up to 10 minutes.

7. Pour the marshmallow into the prepared tray and top with a liberal sprinkling of toasted coconut. Save a small amount of the coconut to use later. Leave the marshmallow to cool and set, preferably overnight.

8. Once set, use your fingers to ease the marshmallow away from all sides of the dish. Turn out the marshmallow onto a chopping board. Cut the marshmallow widthways into strips about 3.5cm (1½in) wide and cut each of the strips into squares. Roll the sticky edges in the remaining coconut, so that the marshmallow squares are completely coated. Serve or bag and give as gifts.

We love Grasshopper Pie so much that we turned it into cupcakes *and* these vibrantly coloured slices. Very moreish, the rich chocolate brownie base and silky chocolate ganache topping make these slices our most chocolaty version of the Grasshopper yet. Using a good-quality peppermint essence or extract will prevent them from tasting artificial.

Grasshopper Slices

MAKES 15-20 BARS

FOR THE BROWNIE BASE

200g (7oz) DARK CHOCOLATE (MINIMUM 70% COCOA SOLIDS)

200g (7oz) UNSALTED BUTTER, SOFTENED

250g (9oz) ICING SUGAR

3 LARGE EGGS

110g (4oz) PLAIN FLOUR

FOR THE MINT GANACHE

250ml (9fl oz) DOUBLE CREAM

1kg (2lb 3oz) GOOD-QUALITY WHITE CHOCOLATE, CHOPPED

2 tbsp PEPPERMINT ESSENCE

1–2 drops GREEN LIQUID FOOD COLOURING

FOR THE CHOCOLATE GANACHE

125ml (4½fl oz) DOUBLE CREAM

270g (9½oz) DARK CHOCOLATE (MINIMUM 70% COCOA SOLIDS), CHOPPED

EQUIPMENT

ONE 23 x 32 x 5cm (9 x 13 x 2in) BAKING TRAY

1. Preheat the oven to 170°C (325°F), Gas mark 3, and line the baking tray with baking parchment.

2. Melt the dark chocolate for the brownie in a microwave-safe dish in the microwave or in a small bowl over a pan of simmering water. Allow this to cool slightly before using.

3. In a freestanding electric mixer with the paddle attachment or using a hand-held electric whisk, beat the butter and icing sugar together until light and fluffy. Add the eggs one at a time, beating well after each addition. Scrape down the sides of the bowl. Add the flour and mix thoroughly. Pour the melted chocolate into the mixture and mix until all the ingredients are incorporated and the batter is smooth.

4. Spoon the brownie batter into the prepared baking tray and smooth it down using a palette knife. Bake the brownie mixture for approximately 35 minutes or until it has a light crust and is cooked through. Set aside to cool completely before adding the topping.

5. To make the mint ganache, in a small pan bring the double cream to a gentle simmer. Place the chopped white chocolate in a medium mixing bowl. Pour the really hot cream over the white chocolate and leave it to melt on its own, then stir continuously until smooth.

6. Leave to settle for a couple of minutes. Stir in the peppermint essence and colouring. Cover with cling film and chill until thick, for approximately 1 hour. Stir occasionally.

7. To make the chocolate ganache, in a small pan bring the double cream to a gentle simmer. Place the chopped dark chocolate in a medium mixing bowl. Pour the really hot cream over the chocolate and leave it to melt on its own, then stir continuously until smooth. Cover and chill until it has thickened slightly, stirring occasionally.

8. To assemble, spread the mint ganache over the top of the cooled brownie using an angled palette knife. Cover with cling film and chill for about 30 minutes or until firm. Once chilled, spread the chocolate ganache evenly over the top of the mint ganache and chill for a minimum of 2 hours, or overnight, until firm. Slice into your desired-size pieces.

Be sure to stir continuously when making this classic fudge or else it will catch on the bottom of the pan and burn. The result should be a fudge that is pale in colour with a lovely soft texture.

Vanilla Fudge

MAKES 16–20 PIECES OF FUDGE

300ml (10½ fl oz) WHOLE MILK

350g (12oz) CASTER SUGAR

100g (3½ oz) UNSALTED BUTTER, PLUS EXTRA FOR GREASING

1 tsp VANILLA EXTRACT

EQUIPMENT

ONE 17.5cm (7in) SQUARE TIN

SUGAR THERMOMETER

1. Lightly grease the tin with butter.

2. In a medium pan, bring the milk, caster sugar and butter to the boil, stirring to melt the butter and dissolve the sugar. Continue to boil for approximately 20 minutes, stirring constantly. The mixture must reach the soft ball stage — 115°C (239°F) on a sugar thermometer. You will need to stir quite vigorously towards the end as the fudge can catch on the bottom of the pan easily. Be careful as the fudge will be very hot at this stage.

3. Once it has reached the correct temperature, remove the pan from the heat and set aside to cool for 5 minutes, then mix in the vanilla extract. The fudge might soufflé up in the pan — this is normal. Beat with a spoon until the fudge has thickened and has lost its glossy appearance.

4. Carefully pour the fudge into the prepared tin and leave it to set completely. Don't put it in the fridge.

5. Turn out the fudge onto a chopping board and portion out into pieces to your desired size.

Better than shop-bought, these pretty pink marshmallows are really fluffy and soft and you will impress everyone with your efforts! There's a lot of whisking required, so you'll get the best results using a freestanding electric mixer — do not attempt by hand.

Home-Made Marshmallows

MAKES 35–40 MARSHMALLOWS

SUNFLOWER OIL, FOR GREASING

1 tbsp ICING SUGAR, PLUS EXTRA FOR DUSTING

1 tbsp CORNFLOUR

25g (1oz) POWDERED GELATINE

125ml (4½ fl oz) HOT (NOT BOILING) WATER

2 drops RED LIQUID FOOD COLOURING (OR OTHER COLOUR OF YOUR CHOICE)

2 LARGE EGG WHITES

500g (1lb 2oz) CASTER SUGAR

EQUIPMENT

ONE 32 x 23cm (13 x 9in) BAKING TRAY

SUGAR THERMOMETER

1. Pour a few drops of sunflower oil into the baking tray. Using your fingers, grease the base and sides of the tray with the oil. Sift together the icing sugar and cornflour. Dust the tin lightly with a small amount of the icing sugar mixture.

2. In a small bowl, dissolve the powdered gelatine in the water. Stir to dissolve the gelatine. Add the red colouring (or any other colour you choose) to this mixture to make the marshmallows pale pink.

3. Pour the egg whites into the bowl of a freestanding electric mixer with the whisk attachment or into a large bowl if using a hand-held electric whisk. Leave these for a few minutes.

4. In a small saucepan, dissolve the caster sugar in 250ml (9fl oz) water, stirring only until the sugar has dissolved. Bring the syrup to the boil. It must boil vigorously and reach 122°C (252°F). A sugar thermometer is essential to do this. Boil until it reaches the hard ball stage on the thermometer. Don't stir while the sugar is boiling.

5. While the sugar is boiling, but before it reaches the required temperature, start to whisk up the egg whites. Whisk until the whites are completely stiff.

6. When the syrup has reached the correct temperature, remove the pan from the heat immediately. Allow to cool slightly, then pour the dissolved gelatine into the syrup. It will bubble slightly. Stir until the mixture is well blended.

Recipe continues ...

7. Turn the mixer or whisk speed to slow with the egg whites still being beaten and very carefully pour the hot syrup into the eggs. The mixture will turn creamy. Once all the syrup is added, turn up the speed and keep beating until the mixture becomes thick, but still pourable — this can take up to 10 minutes.

8. Pour the marshmallow into the prepared tray. Leave it to set for at least 2 hours.

9. Dust a chopping board with the rest of the icing sugar and cornflour mix and lightly coat your knife with some sunflower oil. Carefully turn the marshmallow out of the tin. It might be a bit sticky, so will need a little help. Make sure to coat the surfaces of the marshmallow in the icing sugar mix. Sift over extra if necessary.

10. Cut the marshmallow into squares, re-oiling the knife and dusting the cut edges when needed (probably quite often). Serve or bag and give as gifts.

* To make vegetarian marshmallows, use agar agar instead of gelatine, but be sure to follow the instructions on the back of the packet.

* Try different flavours by adding a small amount of rose water, orange flower water or peppermint essence to your marshmallow mixture before leaving it to set.

These can be shaped to set in a tin, as here, or just placed 'free form' on a large baking sheet. You may use other colours, but we feel red works the best to produce the classic pink and white coconut-ice colours.

Coconut Squares

MAKES 20–25 PIECES

250ml (9fl oz) SWEETENED CONDENSED MILK

250g (9oz) ICING SUGAR, SIFTED, PLUS EXTRA FOR DUSTING

200g (7oz) DESICCATED COCONUT

1–2 drops RED LIQUID FOOD COLOURING

EQUIPMENT

ONE 17.5cm (7in) SQUARE TIN

1. Line the tin with baking parchment and lightly dust with icing sugar.

2. In a freestanding electric mixer with the paddle attachment or using a hand-held electric whisk, mix the condensed milk, icing sugar and coconut together until well combined. Take half of the mixture out of the mixing bowl and spoon into the prepared tin.

3. Add a drop or two of red food colouring to the mixture still in the mixer. Mix well until the coconut ice is an even light pink.

4. In the tin, gently pat the white coconut ice until it is about 1.5cm (⅔in) thick. Top the white coconut ice with the pink, patting it down to match the thickness of the white. Together they should be about 2.5cm (1in) thick.

5. Leave the coconut ice uncovered for a couple of hours, preferably overnight, then cut into 20–25 pieces.

These need to be served immediately so that they don't melt! The frozen chocolate can be made in advance and left, wrapped in cling film, in the freezer, ready for when you want to make them in a hurry. A more child-friendly alternative would be to use milk chocolate instead of dark chocolate.

Frozen Chocolate Sandwiches

MAKES 8–10 SANDWICHES

180ml (6½fl oz) WHOLE MILK

24 WHITE MARSHMALLOWS (ABOUT 180g/6½oz)

300g (10½oz) DARK CHOCOLATE
(MINIMUM 70% COCOA SOLIDS), CHOPPED

375ml (13fl oz) DOUBLE CREAM

20 WAFER BISCUITS

EQUIPMENT

ONE 20 x 30cm (8 x 12in) DISH OR BAKING TRAY

1. Line the dish or baking tray with foil.

2. In a medium saucepan, heat up the milk, marshmallows and chocolate together. Stir until the marshmallows and chocolate have melted. Pour the hot mixture into a large mixing bowl and place in the fridge to cool for 20 minutes.

3. In a freestanding electric mixer with the whisk attachment or using a hand-held electric whisk, whip up the double cream until it reaches soft peaks. Gently fold the whipped cream into the chocolate mixture.

4. Pour the mixture into the prepared dish or tray and cover with cling film. Place in the freezer and leave to freeze completely, for approximately 3 hours.

5. Once frozen, turn it out onto a chopping board and divide it up with a hot knife into 8–10 portions. Lay out 10 wafer biscuits and place a portion of frozen chocolate on each biscuit and then top with another biscuit, making a 'sandwich'.

6. These should be served immediately. They can be served with mixed berries or berry compote.

These sweetly named bear claws are popular in America and are usually found in traditional bakeries or doughnut shops. An easy-to-make version of Danish pastries, they are perfect for breakfast with a strong cup of coffee.

Apple & Almond Bear Claw Pastries

MAKES 6 PASTRIES

FOR THE PASTRY

60ml (2fl oz) WHOLE MILK

60g (2oz) CASTER SUGAR

55g (2oz) UNSALTED BUTTER, PLUS EXTRA FOR GREASING

1 tsp SALT

7g (⅓oz) DRIED ACTIVE YEAST (1 SACHET)

1 LARGE EGG

380g (13oz) STRONG WHITE BREAD FLOUR, PLUS EXTRA FOR DUSTING

FOR THE FILLING

3 MEDIUM BRAMLEY APPLES, PEELED AND CORED

80g (3oz) UNSALTED BUTTER

30g (1oz) RAISINS

100g (3½oz) SOFT LIGHT BROWN SUGAR

1 tsp GROUND CINNAMON

1 tbsp CORNFLOUR

Ingredients continue ...

1. In a small pan, heat the milk until just before boiling. Add the sugar, butter and salt to the hot milk and stir to melt the butter and dissolve the sugar.

2. In a separate bowl, dissolve the yeast in 80ml (3fl oz) warm water and set aside for about 20 minutes or until a light foam has formed on the surface. Then add the egg and yeast water to the milk mixture.

3. Place the flour into a large mixing bowl and make a well in the centre. Pour the liquid into the flour and mix to form a stiff dough. Knead the dough on a lightly floured surface for approximately 5 minutes or until the dough is smooth and even. Place the dough back into the mixing bowl and cover tightly with cling film. Place the bowl somewhere warm and leave the dough to prove (rise) for about 1 hour — it should double in size.

4. While the dough is proving, make the filling. Chop the apples into small pieces. In a medium pan, melt the butter and add the apples, raisins, sugar and cinnamon. Cook the apples until they start to fall apart and are soft.

5. In a small bowl, mix the cornflour with 50ml (1¾fl oz) water. Add the cornflour mixture to the cooking apples and stir constantly while the mixture thickens. Spoon the apple filling onto a tray or plate and allow to cool completely.

6. Once the dough has proved, knock it back and knead lightly to make it smooth and even. Roll the dough out on a lightly floured surface. It needs roughly to be a 25 x 46cm (10 x 18in) rectangle. Trim the edges to give yourself a neat rectangle. Using a sharp knife, cut the dough in half down the centre, then into strips, each about 7 x 22cm (3 x 8½in).

Recipe continues ...

FOR THE TOPPING AND GLAZE

1 LARGE EGG, BEATEN

50g (1¾oz) CASTER SUGAR

50g (1¾oz) FLAKED ALMONDS

200g (7oz) ICING SUGAR

EQUIPMENT

PIPING BAG (OPTIONAL)

7. Place about 2–3 tablespoons of the cooled filling about halfway up each pastry strip. Lightly wet the edges of the pastry with a bit of water. Fold the pastry over the filling, pressing down lightly on the edges to seal the folded side. You don't need to seal the other edges. Trim the pastry again to give a neat edge.

8. Using a sharp knife or scissors, cut four to five 'fingers' in the flap of each pastry parcel. Place the bear claws on two baking trays greased with butter. Wrap the trays in cling film and allow the pastry to rise again for about 20–30 minutes.

9. Preheat the oven to 170°C (325°F), Gas mark 3. When the pastries are ready, lightly brush them with beaten egg and sprinkle with the caster sugar and flaked almonds. Bake the pastries for 20 minutes until they are golden brown.

10. For the glaze, in a medium bowl mix the icing sugar with 2–3 tablespoons of water to form a smooth, runny icing. More sugar can be added to thicken the glaze or water to make it runnier.

11. Allow the pastries to cool slightly before glazing. Drizzle the glaze generously over the tops of the bear claw pastries, either with a spoon or using a piping bag if desired. These pastries are best eaten warm on the day they are made.

These melt-in-the-mouth cookies are an American institution. Bake to a pale colour, but be sure to take out just as the edges turn slightly golden — don't overcook. You can use almonds instead of pecans if you prefer.

Pecan Sandies

MAKES 20–24 COOKIES

FOR THE DOUGH

100g (3½oz) UNSALTED BUTTER, SOFTENED

100g (3½oz) CASTER SUGAR

125ml (4½fl oz) SUNFLOWER OIL

1 LARGE EGG

½ tsp VANILLA EXTRACT

340g (12oz) PLAIN FLOUR

½ tsp BICARBONATE OF SODA

½ tsp CREAM OF TARTAR

½ tsp SALT

100g (3½oz) PECAN NUTS, ROUGHLY CHOPPED

FOR ROLLING AND TOPPING

100g (3½oz) CASTER SUGAR

20–24 WHOLE PECAN NUTS

1. Line two to three baking trays with baking parchment.

2. In a freestanding electric mixer with the paddle attachment or using a hand-held electric whisk, cream together the butter and caster sugar until light and smooth. Add the sunflower oil and mix until well combined. Add the egg and vanilla extract and mix well.

3. Sift in the flour, bicarbonate of soda, cream of tartar and salt. Mix well until a light dough forms. Add the pecan nuts and mix through. Wrap the dough in cling film and place in the fridge to firm up for approximately 30 minutes.

4. Preheat the oven to 170°C (325°F), Gas mark 3. Roll the cookie dough into walnut-sized balls, each about 4cm (1½in) diameter. Completely coat the dough balls in caster sugar.

5. Place the balls on the prepared baking trays, spacing them evenly apart as they spread while baking. Press a whole pecan nut into each cookie. Bake for 10–12 minutes or until the edges are just turning brown. Allow to cool before serving.

Cute little after-dinner offerings that can also be made using mini silicone baking cups. You'll need a sugar thermometer to make your own marshmallow for the filling and an electric mixer as you have to beat the mallow until it doubles in size.

Mallow Cups

MAKES 24 MINI CUPS

3-4 CHOCOLATE COOKIES (SUCH AS OREOS OR MARYLANDS)

200g (7oz) DARK CHOCOLATE (MINIMUM 70% COCOA SOLIDS), CHOPPED

1 tbsp (10g/½oz) POWDERED GELATINE

100g (3½oz) CASTER SUGAR

40g (1½oz) GOLDEN SYRUP

1 LARGE EGG WHITE

PINCH OF SALT

½ tsp VANILLA EXTRACT

EQUIPMENT

ONE 24-HOLE MINI MUFFIN TIN

SUGAR THERMOMETER

PIPING BAG AND A ROUND NOZZLE

1. Line the mini cupcake tin with mini paper cases. In a food processor with the blade attachment, blitz the cookies into fine crumbs.

2. Melt the dark chocolate in a microwave-safe bowl in the microwave or over a pan of simmering water. Using a pastry brush, carefully paint the inside of each cupcake case with the melted dark chocolate. Make sure to evenly coat each case in chocolate. Sprinkle a small amount of cookie crumbs into each chocolate-coated case.

3. Put the tin in the fridge for the chocolate to set. Reserve the remaining melted chocolate to use later.

4. In a small bowl, soften the gelatine in 60ml (2fl oz) hot (not boiling) water.

5. In a medium saucepan, heat the caster sugar, syrup and 30ml (1fl oz) water, stirring until the sugar has dissolved. Bring the sugar liquid to the boil and boil until it reaches the soft ball stage — 115°C (239°F) on a sugar thermometer. Don't stir while the sugar is boiling.

6. While the sugar is boiling, whisk up the egg white using a freestanding electric mixer with the whisk attachment or a hand-held electric whisk until it forms soft peaks.

7. Remove the sugar from the heat when it reaches the correct temperature and leave it to cool for about 3 minutes. Pour the gelatine into the hot syrup, stirring gently to dissolve the gelatine.

8. With the mixer or whisk on a slow speed, pour the hot syrup onto the egg white as it's being beaten. Add the salt and vanilla extract once all the syrup has been poured in — this can be done while the machine is on. Once all the syrup has been added, turn up the mixer speed to high and beat until the marshmallow has doubled in size and is thick.

9. Spoon the soft marshmallow into a piping bag. Carefully pipe about a teaspoon of the mixture into each chocolate case. Set aside for the marshmallow to set. Once the marshmallow has set, re-melt the remaining chocolate if necessary and then top each case with melted chocolate. Allow the chocolate to cool and set before serving. Serve as a treat with coffee after dinner.

Any dried fruits and nuts can be used as a substitute for the almonds, apricots and chocolate. Just keep the weights the same as those called for in the recipe. Don't worry about cutting the brittle into evenly sized pieces — it's impossible!

Apricot & Almond Brittle

MAKES 1kg (2lb 3oz) BRITTLE

180g (6½oz) FLAKED ALMONDS

200g (7oz) DRIED APRICOTS, THINLY SLICED

100g (3½oz) DARK CHOCOLATE CHIPS (MINIMUM 70% COCOA SOLIDS)

600g (1lb 5oz) CASTER SUGAR

400ml (14fl oz) WATER

1. Line a large baking tray with baking parchment and preheat the oven to 170°C (325°F), Gas mark 3.

2. Spread the flaked almonds onto the lined tray and toast them in the oven until they are a light golden colour — this will only take a few minutes. Set aside to cool.

3. Once the toasted almonds are cool, add the sliced apricots and chocolate chips to the same tray and use your hands to mix them in evenly.

4. In a medium saucepan, dissolve the caster sugar in the water. Bring to the boil and continue to boil for 15–20 minutes or until it forms a rich caramel colour. Do not stir while the mixture is boiling or the caramel will crystallise; just gently swirl the pan from time to time.

5. Carefully pour the hot caramel over the nuts, fruit and chocolate, making sure to try and cover all of the ingredients evenly in sugar. Carefully set aside as the tray will be hot, and leave the brittle to cool and set completely.

6. Once cooled, break into pieces and serve or give as a home-made gift.

A wonderfully retro mountain of cold ice-cream and hot meringue. We've used shop-bought ice-cream and the sponge can be made in advance to make it easier to build your own Alaska. If you don't want to bake the pudding in the oven, use a cook's blowtorch instead. And, oh yes, you need to serve this immediately!

Baked Alaska

SERVES 8-10

FOR THE SPONGE BASE
40g (1½oz) UNSALTED BUTTER, SOFTENED

120g (4oz) PLAIN FLOUR

140g (5oz) CASTER SUGAR

1½ tsp BAKING POWDER

120ml (4fl oz) WHOLE MILK

½ tsp VANILLA EXTRACT

1 LARGE EGG

FOR THE FILLING
2 litre (3½ pint) TUB OF ICE-CREAM (ANY PREFERRED FLAVOUR – NEAPOLITAN WORKS VERY WELL)

FOR THE TOPPING
200g (7oz) CASTER SUGAR

100ml (3½ fl oz) WATER

4 LARGE EGG WHITES

Ingredients continue ...

1. Use cling film to line the bowl. Scoop the ice-cream into the bowl, packing it down firmly to fill the bowl. Once all the ice-cream is in the bowl, cover with cling film and place in the freezer for approximately 1 hour for the ice-cream to refreeze into the shape of the bowl.

2. While the ice-cream is refreezing, make the sponge base. Preheat the oven to 170°C (325°F), Gas mark 3, and line the cake tin with baking parchment.

3. In a freestanding electric mixer with the paddle attachment or using a hand-held electric whisk, mix the butter and all the dry ingredients together until they form a crumb-like consistency.

4. In a separate jug, mix together the milk, vanilla extract and egg by hand.

5. With the mixer or whisk on a slow speed, gradually pour half of the liquid into the flour and butter and mix thoroughly until combined. Then raise the speed and beat to make the batter smooth and thick, with no lumps. Scrape down the sides of the bowl as you go. Once any lumps have been beaten out, reduce the speed again and gradually add the remaining liquid, continuing to mix until it is incorporated and the batter is smooth once more.

6. Spoon the batter into the prepared cake tin. Bake for approximately 20–25 minutes or until the sponge bounces back when lightly touched. Take out of the oven and allow to cool completely.

7. For the meringue topping, place the sugar into a small pan and cover it with the water. Heat gently until dissolved, then bring to the boil and allow the syrup to boil, without stirring, until it has reached the soft ball stage – 115°C (239°F) on a sugar thermometer.

Recipe continues ...

ONE 17.5cm (7in) DIAMETER FREEZER-PROOF BOWL
10–13cm (4–5in) DEEP

ONE 20cm (8in) DIAMETER CAKE TIN

SUGAR THERMOMETER

COOK'S BLOWTORCH (OPTIONAL)

8. Meanwhile, using the freestanding electric mixer with the whisk attachment or the hand-held electric whisk, whisk the egg whites until foamy. Once the syrup has reached the correct heat, increase the mixer or whisk speed to medium and carefully pour the hot syrup onto the egg whites in a steady stream. Be very careful as the sugar is extremely hot and will burn if it comes into contact with your skin. When all the sugar has been added, increase the speed to high and allow the meringue to whip up. The bowl will be warm to the touch — whisk until the underside of the bowl has cooled a little but still feels lukewarm. The meringue should have quadrupled in size and become very white and glossy.

9. To assemble the Alaska, line a baking tray with baking parchment and preheat the oven to 200°C (400°F), Gas mark 6. Turn the cooled cake sponge out onto the prepared tray. Take the ice-cream out of the freezer and take it out of the bowl. If it's difficult to remove, sit the bowl inside a larger bowl of hot water until the ice-cream loosens. Turn the ice-cream dome flat side down onto the centre of the cake sponge. There should be about a 2.5cm (1in) border of sponge all around the ice-cream. Remove the cling film.

10. Using a palette knife or a dessertspoon, generously coat the ice-cream with the meringue. Make sure to completely cover the ice-cream and the edge of the sponge in meringue, creating an 'igloo' shape.

11. Place the Alaska in the oven and bake for 10–12 minutes or until the meringue is light brown. If you have a cook's blowtorch, you can brown the meringue that way if you prefer.

12. Place the Alaska straight back in the freezer for another 45–60 minutes to re-set. Try not to leave it in the freezer too long as the sponge will freeze and will not be pleasant to eat. Slice and serve chilled.

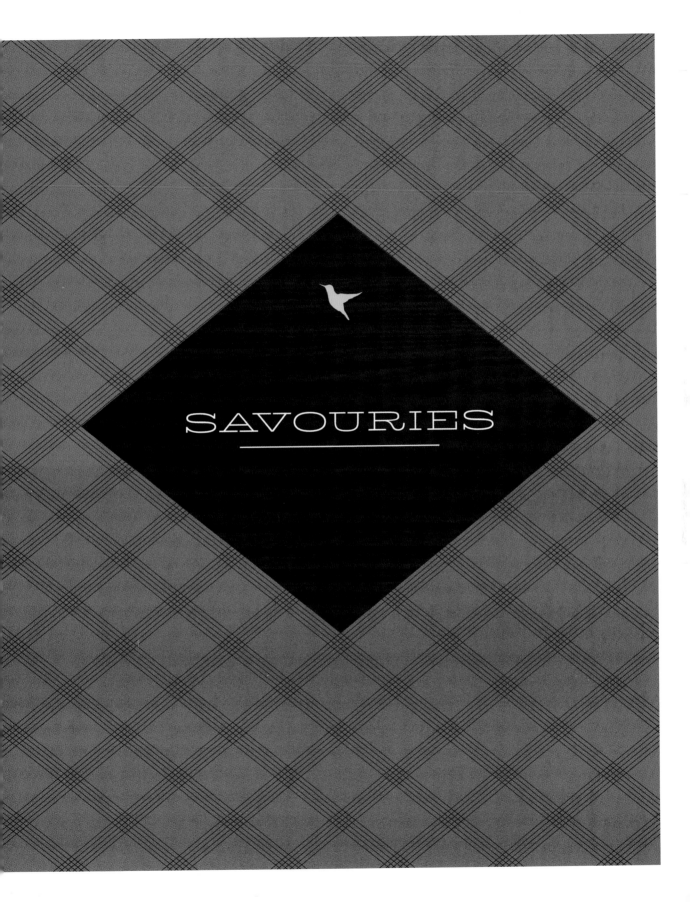

SAVOURIES

Although our bakeries sell only sweet goodies, when we bake at home we love to indulge our savoury tooth too. These Parmesan shortbreads are perfect as finger food for any party. They are best eaten on the day you make them and you can vary the cheese used, just stick to a very hard cheese and keep to the same quantities called for by the recipe.

Parmesan Shortbreads

MAKES 20–30 BISCUITS

125g (4½ oz) PLAIN FLOUR
125g (4½ oz) PARMESAN CHEESE, FINELY GRATED
¼ tsp MALDON SEA SALT
¼ tsp GROUND BLACK PEPPER
¼ tsp CAYENNE PEPPER
100g (3½ oz) COLD UNSALTED BUTTER, CUBED
1 LARGE EGG YOLK

EQUIPMENT

6cm (2½ in) ROUND, FLUTED COOKIE CUTTER

1. Line 2–3 baking trays with baking parchment.

2. In a food processor, mix the flour, grated cheese, salt and spices together. Add the cold butter cubes and process until there are no large lumps of butter and the mix has a sandy texture. Add the egg yolk, and mix until the dough comes together. Roll the dough into a ball, press to flatten slightly, then wrap in cling film and refrigerate for approximately 1 hour.

3. Preheat the oven to 180°C (350°F), Gas mark 4. Roll the chilled dough out on a lightly floured surface to about 5mm (¼in) thick. Using the cookie cutter, cut out the biscuits and place them on the prepared trays, leaving about a 2.5cm (1in) space between each biscuit.

4. Bake the biscuits for about 10–12 minutes or until golden brown. Allow to cool completely before serving.

Cornbread is a great alternative to standard bread for the home baker as there's no proving or kneading involved and it's ready to eat in under an hour. This jazzed-up version of the traditional American recipe can be served warm or cold, and is great with mature Cheddar and apple chutney to accompany.

Chilli Cumin Cornbread

SERVES 8–10

20g (¾oz) CUMIN SEEDS

150g (5½oz) PLAIN FLOUR

1 tsp BAKING POWDER

½ tsp BICARBONATE OF SODA

50g (1¾oz) SOFT LIGHT BROWN SUGAR

60g (2oz) COARSE POLENTA

½ tsp CHILLI FLAKES (CAN BE REDUCED TO SUIT)

1 tsp MALDON SEA SALT

PINCH OF GROUND BLACK PEPPER

2 LARGE EGGS

90g (3oz) SOURED CREAM

100ml (3½fl oz) WHOLE MILK

120g (4oz) TINNED SWEETCORN

EQUIPMENT

ONE 900g (2lb) LOAF TIN

1. Preheat the oven to 180°C (350°F), Gas mark 4, rub the sides of the loaf tin with butter and line the base with baking parchment.

2. In a small dry frying pan, toast the cumin seeds for a few minutes until they are just starting to turn golden and smell aromatic, then remove and leave to cool.

3. Combine all the dry ingredients together in a freestanding electric mixer with the paddle attachment or using a hand-held electric whisk. Mix the eggs, soured cream and milk together in a jug.

4. Add the liquid to the dry ingredients and beat together. Stir in the sweetcorn and toasted cumin seeds.

5. Pour the batter into the prepared loaf tin and place in the oven to bake for 30 minutes or until risen, golden and a skewer inserted into the centre of the loaf comes out clean.

6. Once baked, take out of the oven and leave to cool for a little in the loaf tin, then turn out and serve warm or cold.

We all love cheese straws when they're passed around at parties and they are so cheesy-peasy to make there's no reason to buy them. You can make a variety — sprinkle some with finely chopped walnuts or seeds before baking or vary the cheese used, though it's best to stick to harder cheeses.

Cheese Straws

MAKES 12-14 STRAWS

250g (9oz) READY-MADE PUFF PASTRY

PLAIN FLOUR, FOR DUSTING

1 LARGE EGG

60g (2oz) PARMESAN CHEESE, GRATED

120g (4oz) GRUYÈRE CHEESE, GRATED

1 tbsp FRESH THYME, FINELY CHOPPED

SALT AND GROUND BLACK PEPPER, TO TASTE

1. Preheat the oven to 170°C (325°F), Gas mark 3, and line two baking trays with baking parchment.

2. Roll the puff pastry out on a lightly floured surface. It needs to be a rectangle of roughly 25 x 30cm (10 x 12in).

3. Beat the egg in a small bowl. Gently brush the top of the puff pastry, making sure it is evenly covered in egg.

4. Mix the cheeses, thyme, salt and pepper together in a medium mixing bowl. Sprinkle the cheese mixture evenly over the puff pastry. Using the rolling pin, press the cheese into the pastry.

5. Using a large, sharp knife, cut the sheet crossways into 12–14 strips. Twist each strip and place on the prepared baking trays. Bake for approximately 15 minutes or until golden brown and crispy.

Good-quality olives bought at the deli counter will pack a taste punch for this deliciously easy Mediterranean bread. However, do be sure to check that all the olives you use are pitted.

Olive Loaf

SERVES 8-10

FOR THE DOUGH
600g (1lb 5oz) STRONG WHITE BREAD FLOUR, SIFTED
1 tbsp BAKING POWDER
½ tsp GROUND BLACK PEPPER
⅛ tsp CRUSHED GARLIC
1 tsp MALDON SEA SALT
1 tbsp FINELY CHOPPED FRESH ROSEMARY
2 LARGE EGGS
125ml (4½fl oz) OLIVE OIL, PLUS EXTRA FOR GREASING
250ml (9fl oz) WHOLE MILK
1 tbsp HONEY
200g (7oz) PITTED BLACK OLIVES, ROUGHLY CHOPPED
2 tbsp BLACK OLIVE TAPENADE

FOR THE TOPPING AND DECORATION
½ tsp MALDON SEA SALT
3-4 FRESH ROSEMARY SPRIGS

EQUIPMENT
ONE 900g (2lb) LOAF TIN

1. Preheat the oven to 160°C (320°F), Gas mark 3, and grease the loaf tin with olive oil.

2. In a freestanding electric mixer with the paddle attachment or using a hand-held electric whisk, mix all the dry ingredients for the dough together. In a separate large jug, mix together the eggs, olive oil, milk and honey.

3. Mix the chopped olives and tapenade into the dry ingredients. With the mixer or whisk on a slow speed, pour in the liquid. Mix until all the ingredients are well incorporated.

4. Spoon the dough into the prepared loaf tin. Sprinkle the sea salt over the top of the unbaked loaf and decorate with the rosemary sprigs.

5. Bake for approximately 1–1¼ hours or until a skewer comes out clean of dough when inserted into the loaf. Allow to cool before serving.

Breadsticks are really easy to bake at home from a simple bread dough and make an impressive start to an Italian meal. These breadsticks are crisp on the outside but still soft on the inside and are wonderful served warm. You can roll the sticks in sesame or poppy seeds before baking or use different cheeses to give variety.

Cheese & Rosemary Breadsticks

MAKES 10-12 BREADSTICKS

FOR THE DOUGH

180ml (6½fl oz) LUKEWARM WATER

1½ tsp CASTER SUGAR

1½ tsp DRIED ACTIVE YEAST

210g (7½oz) STRONG WHITE BREAD FLOUR, PLUS EXTRA FOR DUSTING

¼ tsp SALT

FOR THE COATING

80g (3oz) PARMESAN CHEESE, FINELY GRATED

60g (2oz) GRUYÈRE CHEESE, FINELY GRATED

1 tsp FRESH ROSEMARY, FINELY CHOPPED

1 tsp MALDON SEA SALT

¼ tsp GROUND BLACK PEPPER

60ml (2fl oz) OLIVE OIL

1. In a jug, mix the water, caster sugar and dried yeast together. Stir well and then leave it to become slightly foaming on the top. This takes approximately 20 minutes.

2. Using a freestanding electric mixer with the dough hook attachment, mix the flour and salt together. On a slow speed, pour in the liquid. Once all the ingredients are well incorporated, turn the mixer to a medium-high speed and let it mix the dough for a couple of minutes. Turn out onto a lightly floured surface and knead gently by hand until it forms a smooth, even dough.

3. Alternatively, mix the flour and salt in a large mixing bowl, make a well in the middle and pour in the liquid, then mix with a wooden spoon until incorporated. Turn out onto a lightly floured surface and knead the dough with your hands until even and smooth.

4. Place the dough in a large floured or oiled bowl and cover it tightly with cling film. Leave the bowl in a warm location for approximately 40 minutes for the dough to rise.

5. In a medium bowl, mix together the cheeses, rosemary, salt and pepper. Set this aside.

6. Preheat the oven to 180°C (350°F), Gas mark 4, and line two to three baking trays with baking parchment.

7. Once the dough has risen, knock it back in the bowl and turn it out onto a lightly floured surface. Keep it covered with a slightly damp clean tea towel.

8. With floured hands, break off a few small balls of dough at a time and roll them into a sausage shape, about 20–25cm (8–10in) long and about 1.5cm (⅔in) thick. Place the rolled-out pieces of dough on the prepared trays, brush them lightly with olive oil and then sprinkle generously with the cheese mixture. Gently press the cheese mixture onto the dough to help it stick.

9. Bake for 10–15 minutes or until cooked and a golden brown colour.

Yes, it's a savoury cheesecake! If you love our sweet cheesecakes, then this quiche-like version made with Cheddar, basil and green beans is definitely worth a try. This is a baked cheesecake so it can be served warm or cold, but do let it set completely before serving. The vegetables used can be varied according to taste, but stick to the total weights used in the recipe.

Savoury Cheesecake

SERVES 8–10

FOR THE BASE

125g (4½oz) UNSWEETENED WHEAT OR BRAN BISCUITS OR CRACKERS

50g (1¾oz) MIXED SEEDS (SUNFLOWER AND SESAME)

50g (1¾oz) UNSALTED BUTTER, MELTED

FOR THE CHEESECAKE TOPPING

250g (9oz) FULL-FAT CREAM CHEESE (SUCH AS PHILADELPHIA)

300g (10½oz) SOURED CREAM

4 LARGE EGGS

140g (5oz) MATURE CHEDDAR CHEESE, GRATED

10g (1½oz) FRESH BASIL, ROUGHLY CHOPPED

200g (7oz) PEAS

200g (7oz) FINE BEANS

200g (7oz) RUNNER BEANS

SALT AND GROUND BLACK PEPPER

EQUIPMENT

ONE 25cm (10in) DIAMETER SPRING-FORM CAKE TIN

1. Line the cake tin with baking parchment.

2. In a food processor with the blade attachment, blitz the bran biscuits into fine crumbs. Pour the crumbs into a large bowl and combine with the mixed seeds. Stir the melted butter into the crumbs and seeds and mix until evenly coated in butter and the mixture can be squeezed together. Press the crumb base into the prepared tin. Place the tin in the fridge for the base to set for approximately 40 minutes.

3. Preheat the oven to 160°C (320°F), Gas mark 3. In a freestanding electric mixer with the paddle attachment or using a hand-held electric whisk, beat the cream cheese, soured cream and eggs until smooth. Stir in the Cheddar cheese and basil. Season with salt and pepper.

4. Blanch all the peas and beans in boiling water for 3 minutes. Remove from the hot water and cool down immediately under cold running water, then slice the beans. Season the peas and beans with salt and pepper and arrange on the prepared biscuit base, spreading them out evenly. Pour the prepared cheese mix over the top.

5. Bake the cheesecake for 1–1¼ hours or until the cheesecake is set with an even golden brown colour on the top. Allow to cool slightly before chilling completely in the fridge, ideally overnight.

BAKING ESSENTIALS

Baking is a science as well as an art so there are some basic tips and techniques you need to bear in mind before you get started. You'll find lots of useful advice here, including replies to questions that we are frequently asked and other helpful information from our website, hummingbirdbakery.com, and Facebook page. Using this chapter for reference and following the recipes carefully will help ensure your cakes, pies and cookies turn out perfectly each time — as beautifully presented and good to eat as the ones we sell in our bakeries. Above all, we hope you have fun making the recipes. Once you've made a few, you could even try out your own ideas for different flavours, or simply mix and match different cakes and frostings, just as we do at The Hummingbird Bakery.

INGREDIENTS

Quality is key when choosing ingredients for baking. For the best results, buy the best you can afford, and always use full-fat dairy products as the higher fat content is very important for achieving the right texture and flavour.

BUTTER This should always be unsalted, as salt can affect the taste of the finished dish. If you're using it for making a sponge, it needs to be very soft, so take it out of the fridge an hour or so before you start cooking — or soften it for a few seconds in the microwave if you're pushed for time. For pastry, butter is best straight from the fridge as everything needs to be kept cold (see Methods & Techniques/Pastry, page 294). Margarine in a tub has the advantage of being soft already and therefore easy to mix in, although we don't recommend it as a substitute for butter. If you like the taste of a particular margarine or spread, however, then by all means use it if you prefer.

MILK Always use whole milk, as specified in the recipe.

CREAM Double cream is best. If you have to substitute with whipping cream, try to select a brand with a similar fat percentage to ensure that it works equally well in the recipe.

BUTTERMILK Like standard cow's milk, this needs to be full fat in order to work properly. It's available from the dairy aisle of most large supermarkets, although you could try substituting with a mixture of half whole milk and half full-fat natural yoghurt.

CREAM CHEESE We recommend using only full-fat Philadelphia cream cheese as the fat content is crucial in ensuring the recipe turns out correctly, as well as providing a luxurious and creamy taste. For frosting it should be used straight from the fridge or it will make the frosting runny, but this should then be beaten before using to make it softer (see also the tips in Methods & Techniques/Frosting, page 290).

EGGS These should be large, if specified in the recipe, and at room temperature.

COCOA POWDER AND CHOCOLATE Use a really good-quality brand of cocoa powder and good-quality chocolate with a minimum of 70 per cent cocoa solids if you're using dark chocolate. We recommend Green & Black's, but Swiss and Belgian dark or milk chocolate works well so long as you stick to the 70 per cent rule for dark.

FLOUR If a recipe calls for plain flour, never substitute with self-raising flour, as this contains raising agents and will affect the outcome.

BAKING POWDER AND BICARBONATE OF SODA These may only be used in very small quantities, but they are essential for helping a sponge to rise and prevent it being dense and heavy. They are not interchangeable — each works in a slightly different way to create a reaction. Follow the recipe carefully for the right amount, using level spoon measurements. And do check that they don't linger in your cupboard too long or beyond their 'best before' dates or they may not be so effective.

WHITE VINEGAR Used as part of the baking process, the taste won't be detectable in the finished cake. We use distilled white vinegar in our bakeries as we steer clear of alcohol in our products on the counter, but white wine vinegar is fine to use. You can also substitute with white malt vinegar or white cider vinegar, but don't use a dark vinegar as this will affect the flavour.

VANILLA EXTRACT For the best results, it's important to use natural vanilla extract (or 'essence', which means the same thing) rather than an artificial vanilla flavouring. By all means experiment using vanilla pods, if you prefer, but you may need to make a few batches to get the flavour right.

NUTS Toasting or roasting nuts before you use them really improves their flavour. Unless otherwise specified in the recipe, toss them in a small saucepan over a medium-to-high heat for 2–3 minutes. Remove from the heat as soon as they turn brown as they can burn easily.

FOOD COLOURING Liquid food colouring is readily available from any supermarket, but as there are many different brands, all with slightly different colour ranges, you may need to shop around to find your preferred shade. A better colour can usually be obtained from a gel paste, available from cookshops and specialist cake shops or online. You will need less paste than you would liquid; just add a little at a time until you achieve the desired result. A proper deep red, such as for the Red Velvet Roulade (see page 108), is the trickiest colour to achieve. For this a 'non-natural'

red gel paste is best — we recommend the Silver Spoon brand, available from most supermarkets. ('Natural' colourings aren't strong enough to create a good depth of colour, and adding more may just spoil the flavour and cause the batter or frosting to split.)

GLUTEN- AND DAIRY-FREE SUBSTITUTES At Hummingbird we haven't yet found any good substitutes for dairy products or eggs, although do feel free to experiment yourself to see if you can create something to your taste using dairy-free ingredients. You can use gluten-free flour, however, and we'd recommend the Doves Farm range. You can also substitute bicarbonate of soda and baking powder with gluten-free alternatives.

SUGAR SUBSTITUTES Our recipes are intended as indulgent sweet treats, the sugar content being an important element in the baking process. But if you are a confident baker or enjoy experimenting in the kitchen, you could try reducing the sugar or using sugar substitutes.

While most of the ingredients in this book can be bought from a supermarket, you may come across one or two slightly unusual or specialist items. You should find most of these in larger supermarkets or specialist cake stores, but if you don't, then online suppliers who deliver to your door are often the best alternative.

EQUIPMENT

WEIGHING SCALES Measuring with accuracy is really important in baking as the chemical interactions of all the various ingredients are what make your finished sponge or loaf. Digital scales are ideal, therefore, as they give more accurate readings than mechanical ones.

ELECTRIC MIXERS AND WHISKS Making a cake by hand using only a spoon or whisk is very hard, requiring a great deal of time and effort, which is why most of our recipes call for either a freestanding electric mixer (with a paddle attachment, or 'flat beater' as it's sometimes called) or a hand-held electric whisk. Creaming butter and sugar together for a sponge or whipping a frosting to perfection requires a good few minutes of constant beating, which is almost impossible to achieve by hand. Unless you're a very keen baker, there's no need to invest in an expensive mixer, however. Hand-held electric whisks (or hand-held blenders with a whisk attachment) can be bought cheaply from larger supermarkets and are so useful for all types of cooking, not just baking.

BAKING TINS Hummingbird recipes are written with specific tin dimensions in mind, so always use the size of cake tin specified or the cooking time will be affected. Whatever the size of the tin, we recommend you fill it to around two-thirds full. This allows space for the sponge to expand and should help to prevent the mixture from overflowing. Cake tins should be about 5cm (2in) deep.

MUFFIN TINS A deep, 12-hole muffin tin is best for our generous Hummingbird cupcakes, rather than a 'bun' tin, designed for smaller 'fairy' cakes. For the Mallow Cups (page 252) you will need a 24-hole 'bun' or 'mini muffin' tin, however.

STANDARD CAKE TINS Non-stick, loose-bottomed ones are preferable, although you should still always grease or line the tin to prevent the mixture sticking to the inside and make the cake easier to remove when cooked. For sandwich or layer cakes, you will need two to four 20cm (8in) diameter loose-bottomed sandwich tins. Slightly larger round tins (23cm/9in and 25cm/10in diameter) are also called for in this book, and you'll need a 17.5cm (7in) square tin for the fudge recipes (pages 230 and 237).

SPRING-FORM TINS Cheesecakes and more delicate types of cakes need to be made in a 20–25cm (8–10in) diameter spring-form tin or you won't be able to turn them out.

CAKE RING TINS You'll need a non-stick 25cm (10in) diameter ring cake tin for the Cheesecake Swirl Cake (page 95) and Streusel Cake (page 114).

OBLONG BAKING TINS A 32 x 23 x 2cm (13 x 9 x ¾in) Swiss roll tin is required for the roulades in this book, while other sizes of oblong baking tin are used for the various bars and slices.

TART TINS AND PIE DISHES Tarts and pies can be made in a 23cm (9in) loose-bottomed tart tin. We specify a 23cm (9in) diameter pie dish in most of our recipes, leaving the choice of dish — whether glass, ceramic or metal — to you. We recommend a sloping-sided American-style pie dish. Ceramic and glass dishes can be easier to slice and serve from (especially for pies with biscuit bases), but metal pie dishes are better at conducting heat and can help pastry bases to crisp up more quickly.

LOAF TINS All our loaf cakes are baked in a standard 900g (2lb) non-stick loaf tin.

FOIL TRAYS AND PIE DISHES When making bars, slices or pies, you might prefer to use foil trays or foil pie dishes, instead of regular metal tins. These are especially useful if you want to transport the cakes or give them away as a gift. They are available from Lakeland, specialist cake shops and catering suppliers.

PAPER CASES See Cupcakes (page 286).

COOKIE CUTTERS You'll find a range of different-sized cookie cutters useful for cutting out the scones and biscuits in this book. We've specified round cutters on the whole (except for the heart-shaped cutters for the Linzer Cookies on page 128), but you could of course use fluted ones or other shapes if you prefer.

PALETTE KNIFE To achieve the characteristic Hummingbird frosting swirl, a palette knife is essential (see Frosting, page 290). The type of palette knife you choose, whether straight or angled, is entirely up to you — whatever you feel most comfortable using.

ICE-CREAM SCOOP See Cupcakes (page 286).

SUGAR THERMOMETER For making caramels or the various sweet treats in this book, a sugar thermometer is very useful for checking that the mixture has reached the right temperature.

PIPING BAG A piping bag is recommended in a number of recipes in this book, for filling cakes or piping swirls of meringue onto a baking tray. A disposable bag — or baking parchment rolled into a cone and taped together — with a hole cut at the tip to the size specified by the recipe can be just as effective as a standard type of bag with a nozzle.

OVEN All the recipes in this book have been tested in a conventional oven. If you are using a fan-assisted oven (which tends to cook things faster), it's a good idea to read the manufacturer's instruction booklet, which will probably recommend turning down the temperature a little. If you no longer have the oven instructions, we suggest reducing the temperature by 10 per cent.

OVEN THERMOMETER All ovens vary in temperature and many people have 'slow' ovens without even realising it. An oven thermometer is a very useful piece of equipment. It can be permanently hooked into your oven so you can always be sure you are cooking your cakes at the correct temperature.

MEASURING & ADAPTING QUANTITIES

MEASURING It is essential that your measuring is precise, especially for frosting, or the finished cake or other dish may not turn out quite as you hoped or look like it does in the photograph. Measurements are given in both metric and imperial, so that everyone can follow them, no matter what type of oven or weighing apparatus they have. You should always use the same system throughout a recipe, however, and never mix the two. All spoon measurements are level unless otherwise stated, and it's important to stick to this as small variations — such as in the quantity of baking powder or bicarbonate of soda (see Ingredients, page 278) — can make a big difference.

DOUBLING QUANTITIES You can double the quantities given in the recipes, but beyond that we can't guarantee the same results. If you are an experienced baker, you may be able to adjust timings and quantities without too much difficulty, making sure that you stick to the same proportions of different ingredients specified in the recipe.

CONVERTING SMALL CAKES TO LARGE ONES It's possible to convert cake mixture intended for cupcakes into layer cakes and vice versa, although as we haven't tested any tin dimensions other than those in our recipes we can't give specific timings. Filling tins and paper cases two-thirds full will help to prevent the batter from overflowing, however. As a general guide, doubling one of our recipes for 12 cupcakes and dividing it among three 20cm (8in) diameter sandwich tins, then baking for approximately 25 minutes at the same temperature, should turn your cupcakes into a layer cake.

METHODS & TECHNIQUES

SPONGE MAKING

When you're baking a Hummingbird cake, you need to follow the recipe exactly as written. Baking isn't a time for experimenting with different proportions; the wrong balance of ingredients can cause a recipe to fail. Our methods may seem unconventional at times, but they are tried and tested, so trust us! You'll notice that we use a slightly different technique than most recipes for making our sponges, for instance, mixing the butter with the dry ingredients (see opposite page, bottom left image) before combining them with the liquid ingredients (see opposite page, bottom right image). We've found that this gives by far the best results. It's also very important to mix the ingredients thoroughly at each stage, beating the finished batter until it is completely smooth and lump-free. See also the following tips:

SIFTING DRY INGREDIENTS It's good practice to sift flour, cocoa powder and icing sugar before use. This removes lumps and improves the texture of the finished cake. If combining dry ingredients like these, it is easiest to simply sift them together, then mix them by hand with a spoon. (Avoid mixing them with a machine as this raises a dust cloud, sending some of your carefully weighed ingredients up into the air.)

CREAMING When creaming butter and sugar, it should be done for a good length of time — 5 minutes or more — until the mixture is really light and fluffy. It is almost impossible to beat the mixture too much at this stage. However, once the flour is added, beat as little as possible, gently folding or stirring it in until just incorporated, as overbeating the mixture at this point will result in the cake being dense or heavy.

ADDING LIQUID INGREDIENTS When adding liquid ingredients to a cake batter, it is usually best to do this in a couple of batches, pouring in just a bit at a time and mixing well between each addition to properly combine the ingredients. Our sponge batter can be quite runny and may sometimes look a little split, but don't worry — your cake will still turn out beautifully.

COOKING TIMES These can really vary depending on your oven (and also how many items are baking at the same time). Just because the specified cooking time is up, it doesn't automatically mean the cake is done. For every recipe, we give a time range, so use this as a rough guide, checking your cake after the minimum time, but leaving it for longer if it needs more time in the oven, and checking it regularly. Try to avoid opening the oven door until the minimum recommended cooking time, or you risk your sponge sinking.

TESTING WHEN COOKED To tell when your cake is ready, insert a skewer into the middle of it. If it comes out clean, with no mixture stuck to it, the cake is cooked. You should also look to see if it is well risen, springy on top and golden brown (though this last bit obviously depends on the flavour or colour of the cake — for example, a chocolate sponge will never be golden!).

NOT TURNING OUT AS EXPECTED If your cake has sunk too much or appears too thin, then it could be due to the raising agents (bicarbonate of soda and/or baking powder — see Ingredients, page 278) being out of date. Not creaming the butter and sugar for long enough may also be a contributing factor. Equally, if the dry ingredients aren't mixed adequately, this can lead to the sugar caramelising and creating a hard brown top — although it's natural for the top to be a bit drier and crustier than the rest of the cake. It's also common for the top of a cake to crack. If you run a knife around the inside edge of your tin when the cake is straight out of the oven, it will help to prevent the sponge from cracking as it shrinks and cools. Once the cake is frosted, of course, any hardness, overcooked edges or other imperfections will be completely hidden!

COOLING Cakes should be completely cool before you frost or store them. The frosting might melt or slide off the cake otherwise, or the cupcake cases may peel away too readily.

CUPCAKES

PAPER CASES For all our cupcake recipes, we recommend using standard muffin cases as regular cake cases are too small — you will get fairy cakes, not cupcakes. Muffin cases are readily available from supermarkets and there are many brands to choose from. We recommend trying different types until you find a variety that you are happiest with. Some may be more difficult to peel off the finished cupcakes than others, for instance, while some may peel away too easily.

FILLING THE CASES To fill the cases evenly, so that your cupcakes are uniform in size and height, we suggest using an ice-cream scoop to measure an exact quantity of batter each time. You can easily buy a suitable scoop from supermarkets, cookshops or online. The scoop we use holds 50ml (1¾fl oz) of batter, which is just under 4 tablespoons. Of course, you can measure with a tablespoon instead, but this is more long-winded. A less accurate method is to simply fill each case two-thirds full.

USING LEFTOVER BATTER The cupcake recipes all make 12–16 cakes, so you may find that you've filled your 12-hole muffin tin and still have some batter left over. If you own a second tin, fill more cases with the remaining batter and cook at the same time. If you have only one tin, set the remaining batter aside in a cool place, wait until the first batch is out of the oven, remove them from the tin, then fill more cases with the remaining batter and cook a second batch.

BAKING All cupcakes should be cooked on the middle shelf of the oven for 20–25 minutes. Sometimes you may find that your cupcakes rise into peaks, especially if your oven is too hot, but so long as they're light and moist this won't matter at all. You can easily disguise the tops with frosting, or simply slice off the peaks if you find it easier to frost them flat.

FROSTING

When making frosting, don't worry if the proportions seem a little odd or if it takes ages for the butter to incorporate with the icing sugar. It's correct for the mixture to be quite fine and 'sandy'. Once you add the milk, all of a sudden it will begin to come together to make a nice, soft, fluffy icing. It takes a bit longer to make than conventional buttercream icing, but the result is much more delicious. Frosting can be scooped onto cupcakes, preferably using a 50ml (1¾fl oz) ice-cream scoop if you have one (avoid using a spoon as this tends to get messy), and swirled with a palette knife. For the Hummingbird technique, see the step-by-step instructions below.

NOT TURNING OUT AS EXPECTED If your buttercream frosting seems too runny, then you may have added too much milk. Beat again and try adding a little more (sifted) icing sugar until it thickens sufficiently. In the case of a runny cream cheese frosting, you may have beaten the mixture for too long, causing the cream cheese to split. To prevent this happening, beat only for a minute or two once you've added the cream cheese to the icing sugar and butter mixture, just until the frosting reaches the right consistency.

WHITE BUTTERCREAM FROSTING To make frosting that's almost white (or as pale as possible), just keep beating the mixture — the longer you beat it, the paler it will become. We don't use colouring (except by special request for wedding cakes), although for pure white frosting you can purchase a 'whitener' from specialist suppliers.

REDUCING SUGAR If you find the frosting too sweet for your taste, then you can try adding less icing sugar, although this will affect the texture and make the frosting more runny. While we don't recommend recipe substitutions as a rule, you could try experimenting with sugar substitutes or sweeteners if you prefer.

FROSTING CUPCAKES

1. Use a 50ml (1¾fl oz) ice-cream scoop, if you have one, to place a generous amount of frosting on top of the cupcake.

2. With the flat surface of a palette knife, spread the frosting around the top of the cake, smoothing downwards and making sure it covers all the way to the edge of the paper case.

3. Put the flat tip of the palette knife in the centre and move in a circular motion to make an indented swirl in the frosting.

4. To create a pretty peak on top, lift the palette knife upwards at the last second.

5. Now enjoy your gorgeous Hummingbird cupcake with its perfect swirled frosting. If you wish, sprinkle over the decoration of your choice, such as coloured strands.

LARGE CAKES

LAYER CAKES When making a layer cake, you want all the layers to cook and rise evenly. For this, it is best to bake them all on the middle shelf of the oven, so you will probably need to bake in batches, putting two layers in the oven at a time (unless your oven is wide enough to fit more on the shelf).

LOAF CAKES Once cooked, loaf cakes often have that characteristic split running down the centre. But so long as your cake isn't dry as a result of being overcooked, it will be fine.

ROULADES For how best to roll up a roulade or Swiss roll, see the step-by-step photographs on page 110. If you're concerned about the sponge cracking as you roll it up, dampen the tea towel (if using) with water before turning the cake out onto it.

FROSTING LAYER CAKES

1. Place the first layer of sponge on a board or plate. With a palette knife, smooth a generous amount of frosting onto the sponge, making sure it is evenly spread and almost reaches the edges. Place the second sponge layer on top and smooth on the frosting as you did for the first layer.

2. Add the third sponge layer in the same way. (If you're making a four-layer cake, the third sponge layer will need to be topped with frosting and the fourth layer added too.) Then lightly frost the sides of the cake. This is just a 'base coat' to pick up any loose crumbs. Also give the top of the cake a light base coat of frosting.

3. Now frost the sides and the top of the cake again, this time with a thicker layer of frosting; it should be thick enough that you can't see any of the sponge through the frosting.

4. Using the flat tip of the palette knife, add texture to the sides of the cake by either gently pulling the palette knife upwards, from bottom to top, to create lines in the frosting or by pulling the palette knife around the circumference of the cake to create the lines.

5. Again using the flat tip of the palette knife, create the pattern on the top of the cake by starting from the outside edge and pulling the knife over the frosting and into the middle in gentle curved lines.

CHEESECAKES

Cheesecakes can be tricky to get right because they often crack across the top. A good technique to avoid this is to put the cheesecake tin into a 'bain-marie' (water bath) while it is baking (a roasting tin is ideal, filled with water to about 5mm/¼in from the top of the cake tin). This creates moisture in the oven to prevent the cheesecake from drying out and cracking. If you're worried about the tin leaking and water coming into contact with the mixture, wrap the tin with foil before putting it into the bain-marie. Another way to help prevent a cheesecake cracking is to thoroughly grease the tin — the cake shrinks while cooking, so it needs to be free to pull away from the sides. Also, try not to open the oven door during the cooking time as the blast of cooler air can cause the cheesecake to crack.

COOKIES & BISCUITS

CUTTERS See Equipment (page 281) for advice on these.

COOKIES Cookie dough needs to be sticky and firm so that it doesn't spread too thinly when baked — about 5mm (¼in) is ideal. The eggs and sugar should also be well creamed together, for at least 5–7 minutes. If your oven is cooking your cookies a little too quickly, we suggest using an oven thermometer (see Equipment, page 283) to calibrate it correctly. Sticking to the time specified in the recipe should give the best results otherwise. If you like your cookies softer, however, you'll need to take them out a few minutes earlier.

MACAROONS As with any type of meringue, use a spotlessly clean bowl for whipping the egg whites and try not to overbeat them. Once the macaroons are cooked, take care when you're removing them from the baking tray as they can stick and crack easily.

PASTRY

FOR THE BASIC PIE CRUST (including step-by-step photographs), see page 159. In this and other recipes, it's important not to overwork the dough for the pastry or it will become stiff and brittle and create a tough crust when cooked. Handle the pastry as little as possible when you're mixing it and roll it out on a cold work surface. Chilling the pastry in the fridge for 30–40 minutes helps relax the gluten in the dough, making it easier to roll out.

BAKING BLIND In many instances the pie or tart will need to be 'blind baked' before adding the filling, especially if the filling doesn't require cooking itself. To do this, line your tart tin with the pastry and then put it in the fridge to rest for 20–30 minutes. Next, cover it with a sheet of baking parchment and fill with ceramic baking beans (or uncooked dry kidney beans). Bake in the oven at 170°C (325°F), Gas mark 3, for

10 minutes, before carefully removing the baking beans and the paper and baking the case for another 15–20 minutes or until the pastry is cooked through and a light golden colour. (Small individual tarts will need less time.) Allow to cool before adding the filling.

EXTRA TECHNIQUES

MAKING CUSTARD A number of our recipes call for a custard filling or topping in which you make a paste with egg yolks and other dry ingredients before adding to milk and heating in a pan. It's important to keep whisking the mixture as it heats and thickens, and not to overheat it or the eggs may begin to scramble.

MELTING CHOCOLATE For melting chocolate in a bowl over a pan of water on the hob (rather than in a microwave), it's crucial not to let the chocolate get too hot nor to come into contact with water or it will become stiff and grainy. Before you place the bowl on top of the pan, make sure that the water in the pan is hot but not boiling and doesn't come into contact with the base of the bowl. You can remove the pan from the heat before putting the bowl on top, if you prefer.

STORING

All cakes are best kept in an airtight container. Stored like this, layer cakes can last up to 5 days and cupcakes will stay incredibly moist for 2 days. Loaves and other cakes made using fresh yeast are best eaten the same day, however.

FREEZING Cupcakes and layer cake sponges should ideally be baked fresh on the day, but you can freeze sponges, pie crusts and buttercream fillings. We don't recommend freezing other types of fillings or cream cheese frostings, however. Before freezing, it is important to allow sponges to cool completely and then wrap them in cling film or foil, or place in a polythene bag, to protect them from freezer burn. When thawing them out again, allow the sponges to come up to room temperature before you frost them.

MAKING IN ADVANCE Although we'd recommend baking and frosting on the same day, for most recipes you can make the cake mixture in advance and store it in the fridge overnight before baking the next day. Frosting can be stored for around 48 hours in the fridge in an airtight container (to prevent it hardening). Leave it at room temperature for around an hour (still in the airtight container) and then rewhip to fluff it up.

EXTRA TIPS

For the different types of baking tins to use for the various cakes listed below, see Equipment (pages 280–81).

INDEX

ACKNOWLEDGEMENTS

The Hummingbird Bakery is very lucky to have such a wonderful product development team: Emma Power and Heath MacIntyre. Tasting the 100 fantastic recipes in this amazing book has been an exciting pleasure and I'm so grateful to you both for all your hard work – thank you!

Thank you to Lizzy Gray, Helen Wedgewood, Myfanwy Vernon-Hunt and Steve Boggs at HarperCollins, and Kate Whitaker, Liz Belton, Joss Herd and Lucie McKelvie, for making *Home Sweet Home* so stylish yet indulgent. The design and creativity that has gone into making this book extra special has been a pleasure for us all to see at The Hummingbird Bakery.

Thank you to Zoë Waldie for your valuable support and Sue Thedens for keeping a loving yet eagle eye on our fluttering hummingbird!

I am eternally grateful for the amazing people I have worked with and continue to work with at The Hummingbird Bakery. It's not as easy as people think to do what you all do; I'm lucky to have you all.

Finally, thank you to Fouad, Hanan and Juman for always listening.

Collins

First published in 2013 by Collins

HarperCollins*Publishers*
77–85 Fulham Palace Road
London W6 8JB

www.harpercollins.co.uk

10 9 8 7 6 5 4 3 2 1

Photography © Kate Whitaker, 2013
Text © Tarek Malouf and The Hummingbird Bakery, 2013

Editorial director: Lizzy Gray
Project editor: Helen Wedgewood
Design: Myfanwy Vernon-Hunt and Steve Boggs
Food styling: Joss Herd and Lucy McKelvie
Props styling: Liz Belton

Tarek Malouf asserts his moral right to be
identified as the author of this work.

A catalogue record for this book is
available from the British Library.

ISBN: 978-0-00-741359-1

Printed and bound in China by South China Printing Co Ltd.